Damn Good Dogs!

Damn Good Dogs!

*The Real Story of Uga,
the University of Georgia's Bulldog Mascots*

Sonny Seiler & Kent Hannon

HILL STREET PRESS **d** ATHENS, GEORGIA

A HILL STREET PRESS BOOK

Published in the United States of America by
Hill Street Press LLC
191 East Broad Street, Suite 209 | Athens, Georgia 30601-2848 USA | 706-613-7200
info @hillstreetpress.com | www.hillstreetpress.com

Hill Street Press is committed to preserving the written word. Every effort is made to print books on acid-free paper with a significant amount of post-consumer recycled content.

Our best efforts have been used to obtain proper copyright clearance and credit for each of the images in this book. If an unavoidable and inadvertent credit error has occurred it will be corrected in future editions upon notification. Photographers hold copyrights to their work.

Hill Street Press books are available in bulk purchase and customized editions to institutions and corporate accounts. Please contact us for more information.

Text and cover design by Anne Richmond Boston.

Printed in the United States of America.

Library of Congress Cataloging-in-Publication Data

Seiler, Sonny.
    Damn good dogs! : the real story of Uga, the University of Georgia's bulldog mascots / Frank W. Seiler & Kent Hannon.
       p.   cm.
    Includes index.
    ISBN 1-58818-067-0 (alk. paper)
    1. University of Georgia—Mascots—History. 2. Georgia Bulldogs (Football team)—History. I. Title: Real story of Uga, the University of Georgia's bulldog mascots. II. Hannon, Kent. III. Title.
    GV958.U524 S45 2002
    796.332'63'0975818--dc21   2002012899

ISBN # 1-58818-0670-0

10 9 8 7 6 5 4 3 2 1

First Printing

To Cecelia . . . the true mother of all these dogs, who does far too much work and gets far too little credit, this book is lovingly dedicated.

—Sonny and the boys

To my family, . . . the best part of me.

To the Seilers, for trusting me to tell the story of their remarkable family.

And, of course, to Uga, who was No. 1 in the family of animals long before Sports Illustrated *made it official.*

—Kent Hannon

Contents

Prologue

merica always has a favorite animal. With the exception of Secretariat and an animated mouse named Mickey, it's usually a dog. In years gone by, Rin Tin Tin was king of the canines, then Lassie.

But ever since *Sports Illustrated* put his "Churchillian physiognomy" on the cover of the magazine in 1997 and proclaimed him the nation's No. 1 mascot, the entire country—-and, at times, the entire *planet*—has been gah-gah over Uga.

When the current inhabitant of the spiked collar, Uga VI, flew to Washington, D.C., for a political reception in July 2002, the story of this pugnacious pooch upstaging U.S. senators and congressmen made headlines as far away as London. Previously, a photo of Uga VI

nuzzling a baby at Picture Day 1999 appeared in the *Shanghai Daily.* That's *China,* sports fans. And it's just another indication of the wide-scale adoration that's been building for these all-white English bulldogs since Ike was in the White House and Uga's owner, Savannah attorney Sonny Seiler, was still in law school at the University of Georgia.

Now in their sixth decade of service as UGA mascots, these six dogs have a resume so stellar that even summarizing it is difficult. Yes, Uga V's *SI* cover was high cotton, but these dogs are used to occupying center stage. Uga IV is mentioned in one of the most popular books of all time, *Midnight in the Garden of Good and Evil,* and Uga V got to play his famous father in the film version.

"Uga, I'm going to make you a celebrity," said director Clint Eastwood as he wrestled with Uga V on the floor of Sonny's law office prior to filming.

"Excuse me, Mr. Eastwood," said Sonny's wife Cecelia, "but Uga is *already* a celebrity."

Cecelia wasn't bragging, just telling it like it is, what with Uga IV accompanying Herschel Walker to the Heisman Trophy banquet, ESPN kicking off its fall college football coverage with a short film on Uga V, and a TV show about Uga VI helping Turner South win an Emmy.

Uga I wasn't this big a deal when he strolled into his first game at Sanford Stadium back in 1956. But before you knew it, he had his own student ID card, and nearly four decades later Uga V put his inked paw print on the first membership card issued by UGA's

When Georgia players and coaches gather for a team meeting, Uga is there too.

Each mascot has earned an honorary varsity letter.
But Uga VI is the first to do a Coke ad.

Sonny was interviewed at Picture Day 2002 by
(from left) Jeff Dantzler and David Johnston of AM-960/The Ref.

National Alumni Association. Sure, you say, but does Uga have an honorary degree? He does. A varsity letter? That, too. Has he served as grand marshal of the Homecoming parade? Of course. Has he done a Coke ad? He has. Appeared in *Playboy?* Oh yeah. Is his bio in the football media guide longer than the president of the university's? It is.

Speaking of college football, as *Damn Good Dogs!* goes to press, ESPN's six-foot-seven-inch sideline reporter Adrian Karsten is trying to figure out a way to do a feature from *inside* Uga's famous air-conditioned dog house at Sanford Stadium. When TV networks think of you as an icon of college athletics, you know your canine family tree is highly evolved. But for that to happen, you need the support of a human family that, despite living in Savannah, will toss you and your kennel in the car and drive to Athens like it's next door.

"We've done the math," says Sonny, "and—counting home games, away games, bowl games, support for other Georgia athletic teams, and public appearances—we've covered more than 125,000 miles with Uga."

Which means that the dog known 'round the world has circumnavigated the globe five times in support of the University of Georgia.

What the Seilers can't possibly estimate is the number of photographs Uga has posed for over the years.

"If there's someone in Hollywood who's had their picture taken more often than Uga," says Sonny, "they must be a *big* star."

Sonny's comment comes just as he's turning the Seilers' red SUV with the "Uga VI" license plate into the loading dock at the Classic Center in downtown Athens prior to Picture Day 2002.

The line to get to Uga at Picture Day 2001 started in the lobby of Athens' Classic Center and stretched all the way to the stage.

The athletic association's annual late summer fan fest used to be held outdoors at either Sanford Stadium or the practice field on Lumpkin Street. But as the lines for Uga grew longer and longer—and the August heat threatened to wilt the shutterbugs, the Seilers, and Uga—Picture Day was moved to the air-conditioned comfort of the Classic Center.

In 2001, Uga VI was onstage in the 1,100-seat Classic Center theater as a Disney World–like conga line of Georgia fans wound its way down to him from the main lobby.

"It's like waiting in line for Space Mountain," said a man who planned to use a photo of his two daughters with Uga as a Christmas card.

"Picture Day is like Santa Claus at the mall—times 100," says Sonny, who learns, from talking to UGA's sports promotion director Avery McLean, that the initial waiting line for Uga's 1 to 3 P.M. appearance at Picture Day 2002 began forming at 9:30 in the morning.

"We've already sent hundreds of people home," says McLean. "We told them we were sorry, but that there was no way they'd be able to get to Uga by three o'clock."

The enterprise that drew John Berendt's interest in the pages of *Midnight*—the dressing of the dog—is next on the agenda. It's no easy chore getting Uga VI's red Georgia jersey on him—particularly when he's in a non-cooperative mood. After several failed attempts in a hallway, Sonny's daughter Swann shoves the good-natured but rambunctious pooch into a small bathroom. Using the closet-like confines like a bull riding stall, Swann wrestles the sixty-pound youngster into his jersey, pauses momentarily to put herself back together—and then it's show time!

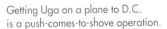
Getting Uga on a plane to D.C.
is a push-comes-to-shove operation.

Passing a table where a Coca-Cola executive has laid out several prototypes of Coke's upcoming ad campaign, Uga VI enters a Classic Center ballroom through a service corridor—and is greeted like a rock star. The crowd of roughly 1,000 people represents a cross section of the Bulldog Nation, but young marrieds with toddlers in collapsible strollers are the most visible contingent.

As Swann places these little tykes at Uga VI's side—a Christmas card in the making every thirty to sixty seconds—an endearing thing often happens: the child kisses Uga or Uga gives the child a great big slobbery lick. Either one produces a collective "Awwwwwwww!" from the crowd.

"People ask me, 'Does Uga bite?'" says Sonny, "and I have a standard answer: 'He never has.' But that doesn't fully describe how loving and tender-hearted these dogs are. My kids have done every rough-house thing you can imagine with these dogs over the course of forty-six years—and Uga has never so much as growled at them."

That's as good a place as any to bring this prologue to a close and send readers to chapter one of *Damn Good Dogs!* If you've ever wondered what the Seilers' personal Uga scrapbook looks like, this is it!

—Kent Hannon

Uga I
1955–67

Born
December 2, 1955

AKC registered name
Hood's Old Dan

Dates of service
October 6, 1956
to October 22, 1966

Football record
52-47-6

SEC titles
1
1959 (10-1)

Bowl record
2-0
beat Missouri 14-0
in '60 Orange Bowl

beat Texas Tech 7-0
in '64 Sun Bowl

Died
November 9, 1967

Epitaph
"Damn Good Dog"

Uga I

The Dynasty Begins

In 1956, The Varsity restaurant was still located in downtown Athens across the street from the Arch, meaning University of Georgia students could work up a good case of heartburn between classes. The university was a much different place back then. Enrollment was only 6,000, making it feel more like a small college. It looked like one, too. The Georgia Center was just a construction site. Sanford Stadium had no upper deck. The Coliseum didn't exist. Students were different, too. Pinnings were announced in the campus newspaper, though some were already history by the time the once-a-week publication hit the streets. The '56 Homecoming act was Sammy Kaye and his Swing and Sway Orchestra. Fountain cokes at the Co-op cost a nickel. And the record students wore out on the Co-op jukebox was "Sixteen Tons" by Tennessee Ernie Ford.

Uga I started the dynasty, he served longer than any of the other mascots—and it all began with a belated wedding present to the Seilers.

Signs of the times: In 1956, The Varsity was still located in downtown Athens across from the Arch, and fountain cokes at the Co-op were only a nickel.

"We had no idea what the Elvis craze was about . . . and we didn't care," says Sonny Seiler. "I guess it was because we felt like we already had just about everything we needed."

Sonny was a student at the University of Georgia in 1956, and he was happy with his lot in life. Born and raised in Savannah, the son of a grocer and a school teacher, he had married his college sweetheart, the former Cecelia Gunn of Columbus, Georgia, the previous November. When Sonny returned to Athens in September for his second year of law school, he and Cecelia moved into an apartment near the Chi Omega sorority house, where she was a member.

Sonny Seiler was a second-year student at the University of Georgia law school in 1956. He was married to the former Cecelia Gunn of Columbus, Georgia, who had started her college career at Mary Washington in Fredericksburg, Virginia, then transferred to UGA.

"We were excited to have a place of our own," says Cecelia. "It was just the two of us back then, and, like any married couple, we enjoyed our privacy—which was very quickly a thing of the past."

It started with a phone call to the Seilers' apartment.

When Cecelia picked up the phone, she expected to hear her husband's voice on the other end of the line asking what was for dinner. The call, in fact, had nothing to do with dinner. And though they didn't know it at the time, the Seilers' lives were about to be changed forever.

Destined for success

That he would be a success in life was a foregone conclusion to anyone familiar with the strength of Sonny Seiler's resolve. For those who didn't know him, the proof was right there in the pages of UGA's *Pandora* yearbooks, which in the mid-fifties were filled with the exploits of Frank W. "Sonny" Seiler:

Sigma Chi fraternity member and president. Interfraternity Council president. Phi Delta Phi legal fraternity. Greek Horseman. Sphinx Society. Gridiron. Omicron Delta Kappa. G-Club.

Uga I

..... A world in which we wide

Sonny got his varsity letter on the swimming team, where he displayed an unusual combination of speed and endurance by competing in both the 50- and 1,500-meter freestyle events. To stay in shape one summer—and to prove to themselves that they could do it—he and Georgia teammate Jack Schaaf slipped into the Savannah River off East Broad Street in downtown Savannah and swam all the way to Tybee Island. Distance: Eighteen miles.

When his collegiate swimming career ended, Sonny went to work for the UGA athletic department. The job was made possible by Georgia's long-time football coach Wally Butts, who arranged for Sonny to spend his afternoons working at the ticket window in old Stegeman Hall—the World War II naval training building, located between Sanford Stadium and Lumpkin Street, where the athletic department was headquartered in those days.

"I made a grand total of thirty-five bucks a week," says Sonny, who would one day rise to the presidency of the Georgia State Bar, "but I remember telling people that I enjoyed the work because selling football tickets helped me stay close to Georgia athletics."

Sonny was all-everything in college: president of Sigma Chi and the Interfraternity Council. (That's him, second from left, in both the above photo with Dean Tate and in the photo at left with the sweetheart of Sigma Chi.) He was also a member of Sphinx, Gridiron, Greek Horsemen, Omicron Delta Kappa, and G-Club. He earned his varsity letter in swimming—and on game days at Sanford Stadium (see below), he blew a mean bugle.

Uga I

Those proved to be prophetic words, because—with the possible exception of an athletic director, coach or player—no civilian, if you will, has been closer to Georgia athletics or done more to celebrate and support the university as a whole over the last half-century than Sonny Seiler.

"Sonny's a fine attorney," says UGA athletic director Vince Dooley, "but he does so much for us that I sometimes wonder how he has time to practice law. I can't think of anyone who has been a better friend to the University of Georgia."

our experiences

Homecoming floats were more elaborate in the 1950s, including this one from the Sigma Chi fraternity, where Sonny Seiler served as president.

Gift that would keep on giving . . . and barking

Sonny was sitting in his usual spot at the ticket window in Stegeman Hall when Cecelia answered the phone back in '56. But it wasn't Sonny who was calling. It was Cecelia's mother with news of a belated wedding present for the newlyweds.

"My mother told me that a friend of ours, Frank Heard, wanted to give us an English bulldog," Cecelia recalls. "In the beginning, I don't think Sonny was too happy about the idea of us having a dog. But I was thrilled!"

Sonny begs to differ with his bride.

"I was just as thrilled as Cecelia," he says. "But we were your typical starving newlyweds—only I was in law school, so that made it worse. We didn't have enough money to feed ourselves, let alone a bulldog."

To help make ends meet, the Seilers ate a lot of Campbell's vegetable soup back in those days. But difficult economic times weren't about to stand in the way of a present this special.

"We couldn't pass up the opportunity to own a bulldog, which symbolized Georgia athletics," says Sonny. "Particularly *this* bulldog."

Uga I

The only survivor of a litter of three, the puppy's bloodlines were of historical significance to UGA diehards like the Seilers. He was said to be the grandson of a white English bulldog who had accompanied the Georgia football team to Pasadena, California, for the 1943 Rose Bowl. On New Year's Day—with World War II raging in both Europe and the Pacific—Charley Trippi and Frank Sinkwich led Georgia to a 9-0 shutout win against UCLA. For nearly four decades, that Rose Bowl victory would stand as the crowning moment in Georgia football history because it enabled the Dogs to finish the 1942 season 11-1 and earn their first National Championship.

"So it was settled," says Sonny. "We were going to take the puppy."

The Seilers got Uga I as a belated wedding gift from a friend of Cecelia's family.

Uga I's bloodlines were of historical significance to UGA diehards like the Seilers. He was said to be the grandson of a white English bulldog, who accompanied the Georgia football team to the 1943 Rose Bowl in Pasadena, California. Georgia shut out UCLA 9-0 that day to win its first National Championship.

Cecelia's sister Sara and her husband, Hersey Sumner, drove from Columbus to Griffin, Georgia, where the Seilers picked up the new arrival.

"He was far from gift-wrapped!" says Sonny, who remembers the little four-month-old pup as clumsy and rambunctious. "To my dismay, he didn't look anything like what I expected. He was tall and gangly. What we had envisioned was a heavy, wide-shouldered bulldog—like the hood ornament on a Mack truck."

When Uga I was a puppy, he was gangly and rambunctious, but he soon grew into a prototypical English bulldog with a proud head and a barrel chest. Here he poses with cheerleader Hannah Jones.

Icon of British Empire and Bulldog Nation

Master, this is your servant
He is rising eight weeks old,
He is mainly head and tummy,
His legs are uncontrolled.
But thou hast forgiven his ugliness,
And settled him on they knee,
Art thou content with they servant:
He is very content with thee.

—Rudyard Kipling, paying tribute
to the English bulldog

With a family tree that can be traced all the way back to 54 B.C., when Julius Caesar invaded England, English bulldogs were originally bred to fight chained bulls of the steer variety. Gamblers wagered money on which bulldog could sink its teeth into a bull's flesh (bears were also a common opponent) and bring the animal to its knees. The overdeveloped underjaw and pronounced underbite were, in fact, necessary to produce the vise-like grip required for bulldogs to have a chance to come out a winner in these violent "sporting encounters" with animals forty times their weight. In 1773, legislation was passed banning public baiting in England, but the practice is said to have continued more or less privately until 1836. A century later, cartoonists wrapped a bulldog in a Union Jack to symbolize England, and World War II caricaturists delighted in exploiting the facial resemblance between the English bulldog and Winston Churchill.

In recent years, the United States has emerged as the bulldog capital of the world, with more than twice as many dogs registered with the Bulldog Club of America as with its counterpart in Great Britain. For the year 2000, English bulldogs ranked a respectable twenty-first in popularity among 148 breeds registered with the American Kennel Club in New York. The Labrador retriever was the runaway winner for most popular dog in the U.S. with 172,841 cumulative AKC registrations—nearly three times as many as the second-place golden retriever with 66,300. With a healthy increase of 1,461 registrations (11 percent) over their '99 total, bulldogs numbered 15,215—ahead of such perennial favorites as basset hounds, Doberman pinschers, Pekingese, and collies.

In a story titled "The Bulldog: A Mellow Fellow," *Dog World* magazine observed that "This sportsman of old has developed into a lovable companion . . . A wrinkled dog of brute strength, unparalleled courage, and bullheaded stubbornness, the bulldog's creased face can break into a doggie grin that will melt any disbeliever's heart."

"I knew the English bull was a revered breed," says Sonny, "and I was predisposed to like them because of their affiliation with my alma mater. I guess that's why I was surprised—and a little disappointed—when I first saw that awkward puppy of ours back in '56."

But even then, he had a plan.

"From the git-go," says Cecelia, "Sonny Seiler had it in his mind that some day this might be *the* Georgia mascot."

Uga I

AMERICAN KENNEL CLUB'S MOST POPULAR BREEDS

AKC registrations / 2000

1.	Labrador retriever	172,841
2.	Golden retriever	66,300
3.	German shepherd	57,660
4.	Dachshund	54,773
5.	Beagle	52,026
6.	Poodle	45,868
7.	Yorkshire terrier	43,574
8.	Chihuahua	43,096
9.	Boxer	38,803
10.	Shihtzu	37,599
11.	Rottweiler	37,355
12.	Pomeranian	33,568
13.	Miniature schnauzer	30,472
14.	Cocker spaniel	29,393
15.	Pug	24,373
16.	Shetland sheepdog	23,866
17.	Miniature pinscher	22,020
18.	Boston terrier	19,922
19.	Siberian husky	17,551
20.	Maltese	17,466
21.	**BULLDOG**	**15,215**
22.	Basset hound	14,427
23.	Doberman pinscher	13,874
24.	German shorthaired pointer	13,224
25.	Bichon frise	11,750
29.	Pekingese	9,749
34.	Collie	8,042
49.	Dalmatian	3,084
72.	Jack Russell terrier	1,488
148.	English foxhound	17

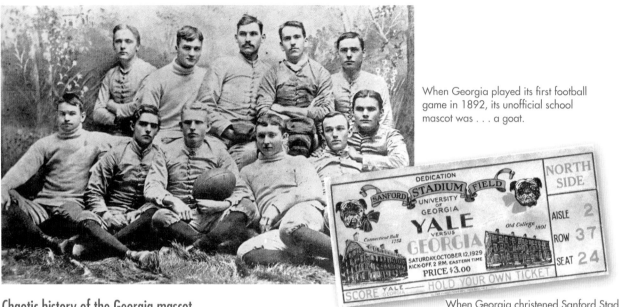

When Georgia played its first football game in 1892, its unofficial school mascot was . . . a goat.

When Georgia christened Sanford Stadium with a 15-0 victory over mighty Yale on October 12, 1929, it pitted the Bulldogs against the Bulldogs.

Uga I

Chaotic history of the Georgia mascot

When the University of Georgia played its first intercollegiate football game, against Auburn on February 22, 1892, its unofficial mascot looked considerably less imposing than the Seilers' gangly pup.

It was a goat.

Newspaper clippings indicate that this nameless, bleating sideline symbol wore a black coat with red "U.G." lettering on each side. Nothing wrong with that outfit, but you have to wonder what UGA students were thinking when they added a little hat to the ensemble and strung ribbons from the animal's horns. Auburn fans reacted predictably, chanting throughout the game, "Shoot the billy-goat!"

No one did, but two years later Georgia was represented on the football field by a white bull terrier named Trilby, who was the mascot of the Chi Phi fraternity. Trilby was a regular at Georgia football practices, and after she delivered a litter of thirteen the players were so taken with her pups that on game days they decorated them with red-and-black ribbons. Trilby's owner, a student from Atlanta named Charles H. Black Sr., always claimed that Trilby and her pups were the origin of the Bulldog nickname.

But bull terriers are not bulldogs—they're a completely different and much more diminutive breed—and Charles Black's version of the mascot's history is just one of many that have been uncovered over the years.

The first mention of bulldogs in the press came on November 29, 1901, when an *Atlanta Constitution* account of the Georgia-Auburn football game noted that "when the Georgia rooters arrived in Atlanta, nearly every one of them had a badge saying, 'Eat 'em Georgia' and a picture of a Bulldog tearing a piece of cloth."

In the February 11, 1938, issue of *The Red & Black,* UGA law professor Robert McWhorter said Georgia teams were called bulldogs when he was in school back in 1914. But in that same *Red & Black* story, former football coach H.J. Stegeman noted that for two years in the 1920s, "Georgia had a basketball team of small but scrappy players called the Wildcats, and the papers kidded the squad so much it had to change the mascot."

To end the debate once and for all, McWhorter—who later taught Sonny Seiler—proposed that the bulldog be officially designated as the school mascot with a "coronation at the biggest game next fall for a live beast which would wear the University colors at every game henceforth."

And so, at halftime of the '38 Homecoming game against Georgia Tech, a bulldog was crowned instead of a Homecoming queen. Formerly known as "Count" but renamed "Georgia" in deference to the occasion, the dog reigned for only one year and was eventually succeeded by Butch after a gap of eight years.

Butch was owned by Mabry Smith of Warner Robins, who loaned the dog to the university after students attending the 1946 Georgia Tech game in Athens spotted the brindle-colored pooch and took a liking to him. Butch served from 1947–51, his tenure ending sadly during the off-season when a policeman inexplicably shot him after he escaped from his pen and was found wandering the streets of Warner Robins.

Mike, who succeeded Butch, served from 1951–55. He, too, was a brindle, and, like Butch, he served with only modest fanfare. Mike lived on South Campus in the attic of the old fieldhouse, which was later known as Alumni House. Some people thought he belonged to Coach Butts. But Mike's owner was actually C.L. Fain of Atlanta, and the athletes who lived in the fieldhouse were the ones who took care of him.

Mike died of natural causes in 1955, but not before serving as a model for art student Gene Owens, whose master's degree project was a 700-pound bulldog statue that still sits on a pedestal outside Memorial Hall. Owens got the idea for the bronze statue from UGA's dean of students Joe Williams and art department head Lamar Dodd. Owens worked on the project ten to twelve hours a day at a bronze works in Gainesville, Georgia. To make sure he got the look just right, he also studied a bulldog skeleton procured from the UGA vet school.

With the demise of Mike, Georgia football coach Wally Butts asked Georgia's sports information director, Dan Magill, to be on the lookout for a replacement for the 1956 season.

BUTCH ON SIDELINES DURING FOOTBALL GAME
Owner Threatens Suit in Death of Bulldog Mascot

GEORGIA'S BULLDOG SHOT at least? 1951

Mascot's Owner Growls Over Death

WARNER ROBINS, Ga., June 7—(AP)—In life—four years of it at least—he pranced proudly before cheering thousands at Athens' Sanford Stadium, home of the famed University Bulldogs.

And Butch, the brindled English Bulldog mascot, stirred as bitter a battle in death today as any he presided over on the gridiron.

He was shot down on the street here and his body was cast onto the city dump.

So his owner, Mabry Smith, is asking City Council to replace his proudest possession, pay the damage or face a suit in court.

Butch was shot to death this past Saturday when he was found roaming the streets after escaping from his pen at the Smith home on Hawkinsville Rd.

Smith, owner of Butch, rabid University of Georgia fan and lover of bulldogs—particularly Butch—says the shooting was not justified.

Butch became the university mascot when he was spotted by students while attending the 1946 Georgia-Georgia Tech game with Smith. The university needed a mascot, so Smith agreed to loan them Butch during the football season along with a female puppy named Tuffy.

The female died of a heart attack following the University of Georgia-Kentucky game in 1948. Butch has continued to serve as mascot since the 1947 season. During the off season, he spent his time with Smith at Warner Robins.

SMITH TOLD council members that a friend called him Saturday afternoon to tell him he saw Butch roaming the streets. He said he immediately started a search for the dog and learned Butch had been picked up in a police car.

"I called the police department," Smith told council members, "and they informed me he had been shot. I was shocked, naturally, for Butch isn't a vicious dog and had been innoculated, so I asked why it was necessary to shoot him. They told me he was

COPS SHOOT BULLDOG MASCOT; OWNER THREATENS TO SUE CITY

WARNER ROBINS, June 6—(AP)—Mabry Smith has asked the Warner Robins City Council to either reimburse him for the loss of Butch, his English brindle Bulldog who has been University of Georgia mascot the past four years, or prepare to fight a damage suit.

Butch was shot by a policeman Saturday when found roaming the streets. He had escaped from his pen at Smith's home.

Smith said he learned Saturday that Butch was loose, and started searching for him. When he learned that he had been picked up in a police car, Smith said, he called the police department "and they informed me he had been shot.

"I was shocked, naturally, for Butch isn't a vicious dog and had been inoculated, so it was necessary to shoot him. They told me he was suffering so badly from distemper that they just put him out of his misery."

AN EAR TO THE GROUND
ED DANFORTH
SPORTS EDITOR

——These days when beauty contests are bringing pictures of ravishing damsels to promoter's desks, another "beauty" contest is in progress. . . . Candidates for mascot for the University of Georgia Bulldogs are coming to W. O. McDowell, Athens Touchdown Club committee chairman, whose organization will purchase the new dog . . . "Butch," for four years the symbol of Georgia football teams, was picked up by a policeman at Warner Robins, Ga., and shot because he had distemper. . . . The policeman did not know that all bulldogs wheeze that way and he probably had heard dogs with distemper were given "shots."

NEW MASCOT 1951 FOR BULLDOGS TO BE PICKED

Special to Atlanta Journal-Constitution

ATHENS, June 9—Georgia's Bulldogs will have a new mascot next fall. The Athens Touchdown Club is planning a contest to select one to replace Butch, veteran of four seasons, who was shot by a Warner Robins policeman last week.

W. O. McDowell, Touchdown Club president, said the deadline for entries in the contest will be Sept. 1. The winner will make his debut during halftime ceremonies at the Georgia – George Washington game Sept. 22.

Entries must be turned in to McDowell and should include pictures. The canine selected for the new mascot will be owned by the Athens Touchdown Club.

One of Uga I's predecessors was Butch, a brindle-colored bulldog, who served from 1947–51. He met an untimely end when a policeman in his hometown of Warner Robins inexplicably shot him after he escaped from his yard and was found roaming the streets.

Mike served as a model for this 700-pound statue—
cast by art student Gene Owens—
which keeps watch on Memorial Hall plaza.

Uga I

Uga I

Mike, a brindle-colored predecessor of Uga, served as Georgia's mascot from 1951–55. Wielding the leash is "Miss Pandora" Carol Ann Connor.

Uga I became such an instant fixture at Sanford Stadium that the opening pages of the '57 yearbook ran this photo of him with an admiring youngster. He even had his own college ID card.

Uga gets his name

By the time the '56 football season rolled around, the Seilers' skinny white puppy had grown into a prototypical English bulldog with a proud head, a barrel chest, and—as is also prototypical of today's bulldogs—an unmistakable gentleness and affinity for people that belied his ferocious looks.

"He was the real deal, and we felt like we were the envy of our friends and neighbors," says Sonny, whose classmate Billy Young had shared an intriguing idea with him one morning over coffee at the UGA Co-op.

"Seiler, if I had that bulldog puppy," said Young, "I'd name him *Uga*."

"Uh-guh?" said Sonny, who was thinking phonetically, not institutionally.

"Yeah, you know," said Young, "a takeoff on UGA."

In an instant, Sonny went from not understanding what Young meant to thinking he'd come up with the perfect name for their new pet.

"We loved it!" says Sonny. "And that's how Uga got his name."

A mascot needs a jersey, too

In the 1950s, the most popular Georgia football car emblem was a fierce-looking white bulldog in a red sweater with a "G" on the front and a little cap on his head. Borrowing that idea, Cecelia went to the J.C. Penney store in downtown Athens and bought a red Buster Brown T-shirt—children's size 8—for Uga.

"I cut a 'G' out of a piece of black felt," Cecelia recalls, "then sewed it on the chest of the shirt and gathered the sleeves and the waist with elastic. When we put it on Uga, he looked like he'd stepped right out of that Georgia car decal!"

22-A The Atlanta Journal AND CONSTITUTION SUNDAY, SEPTEMBER 30, 1956
King Football Retakes Athens

CHEERLEADERS JUDY JENKINS, LEFT, GAIL HEARD HOLD A FEROCIOUS BULLDOG IN TOW

This newspaper photo of Uga I's first appearance at a Georgia football game on September 29, 1956, caught the eye of university officials who were on the lookout for a new mascot. Fortunately, the caption—which incorrectly described Uga as a "ferocious bulldog"—didn't dissuade sports information director Dan Magill from recommending Uga to Coach Wally Butts.

On Saturday, September 29, 1956, prior to Georgia's first home game of the season against Florida State, the Seilers dressed Uga in the jersey Cecelia had made for him and took him to Sonny's fraternity house on Lumpkin Street for a pre-game party.

"It was mainly for our own entertainment. We never intended to take Uga to Sanford Stadium that day," Sonny recalls. "But he created such excitement at the Sigma Chi house that, when it was time to go to the game, everyone agreed that Uga should go, too."

The Seilers walked Uga to Sanford Stadium for his first college football game, and the ticket-takers were so enamored with his pugnacious attitude and the big "G" on his chest that they waved him through the gate as though he were the team's official mascot.

Which, of course, he wasn't. Not yet, anyway.

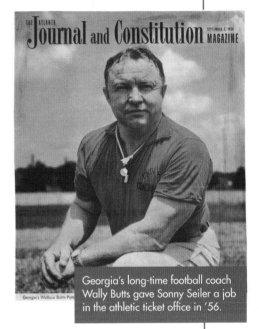

The Atlanta Journal and Constitution MAGAZINE

Georgia's Wallace Butts Puts

Georgia's long-time football coach Wally Butts gave Sonny Seiler a job in the athletic ticket office in '56.

Uga I becomes the official school mascot

"I had placed stories in the newspaper saying the university was shopping for a new mascot," recalls Dan Magill, who found the bulldog he was looking for in newspaper photos from the '56 Florida State game, which served as Uga's audition for the job.

"We never took him on the field that day," Sonny recalls, "but he created a lot of excitement in the stands. Photographers took pictures of him and one ended up in the paper—which attracted the attention of Dan Magill."

Never one to miss an opportunity for publicity, Magill had some photos made of Uga and, unbeknownst to the Seilers, he told Coach Butts that Uga would make a good team mascot.

A few days later, when Sonny reported to work at the ticket office, his immediate boss, Virginia Whitehead, handed him a note that read:

"Coach Butts wants to see you in his office."

Sonny couldn't imagine what was up, but he feared it wasn't good.

"I remember thinking, *What have I done to get fired?*" says Sonny, who went directly to Coach Butts's office on the second floor of Stegeman Hall. The look on Coach Butts's face put him instantly at ease.

"Sonny, Dan tells me you've got a white English bulldog that would make a good mascot for the team," said Coach Butts. "What would you say to us using him to create some excitement?"

Needless to say, Sonny was delighted, and from that simple conversation emerged a line of bulldog mascots that has now stretched into its sixth decade.

Uga was like the Seilers' first child

From that day forward, Uga I or one of his five descendents have attended all home football games and most of the away games. The dogs were an instant hit with Georgia fans, as well as with the cheerleaders, who were responsible for taking care of Uga on the sidelines (see p.13) until the Seilers' fourteen year-old son Charles took over during Uga III's tenure.

As the mascots' fame evolved over the years, Uga would become so endemic to college sports that he would grace the cover of the nation's most prestigious sports magazine, *Sports Illustrated,* which named him the No. 1 mascot in the country. But around the Seiler household, Uga has always been, first and foremost, a beloved pet and member of the family.

"I had Uga I before I had my first child, so he was really like a child to us," Cecelia recalls. "When I was pregnant with our first child, Swann, Uga would sit in my lap. Then when I brought her home from the hospital, he got very upset with all the attention I was giving her and wouldn't have anything to do with me. Bulldogs are

Sonny and Cecelia as young marrieds at the Debtor's Ball in Savannah. He went as a magician who had pulled a Playboy bunny (Cecelia) out of a hat.

very sensitive animals—and they have great memories."

The division of labor in the Seiler family with regard to Uga is very clear-cut.

"Mama is their mother," says Swann, who is now manager of corporate communications for Savannah Electric. "She feeds the dogs, bathes them, and takes them to the vet. Charles is their handler. He's the one you see with Uga at Sanford Stadium. I'm the press agent, I guess, because I work with Uga at things like the picture-taking sessions at Media Day. And Daddy is the owner-manager-agent who promotes Uga and sets up his appearances."

Cecelia may be the mother figure, but Sonny is the dogs' favorite—a trait that has been passed along as faithfully as if it were part of the dogs' gene pool.

"Daddy is gone a lot because of his legal practice," says Swann, "but he has this persona that the dogs really identify with. I can be playing with Uga, or maybe Mama has just given him his food, or Charles is cooling him off on the sidelines at Sanford Stadium. But if Uga catches sight of Daddy—coming up the driveway or clear on the other side of a football field—he wants to go to him."

HOLY BIBLE

FRANK WILKIN

"We didn't realize how jealous Uga was of our first-born," Sonny recalls, "until Cecelia and I took baby Swann with us to the drive-in movie one night. When we got home, Uga had chewed up this small Bible that we kept by our bed."

Before Charles Seiler was old enough to tend to the mascots, they were the cheerleaders' responsibility: Uga I with cheerleader captain Nancy Butts, daughter of the head football coach; with cheerleader Ronny Coven; surrounded by beautiful girls of all ages; and riding a float.

Uga I

Uga is just like another sibling to the Seiler children.

"In the beginning, I didn't really understand the mascot thing," says Swann, who was born on June 2, 1956—two months after Uga I arrived in the Seiler household. "Uga was like a brother to me. He slept with me in our house on Fiftieth Street, we played together in the yard, and I shared my popsicles with him."

On November 15, 1960—nicely timed to coincide with the football team's off-week prior to beating Georgia Tech 7-6 in Wally Butts's farewell game as Georgia's coach—Cecelia gave birth to Charles. Like older sister Swann, his childhood memories are filled with Uga stories.

"One of my earliest memories," says Charles, now a bonding agent for Palmer & Cay in Savannah, "is a picture of me with my dad and Uga I at Halloween. All my friends were wearing Batman and Superman costumes that year, but I went trick-or-treating in a Georgia football uniform. I even had the shoe polish under my eyes, and I remember carrying a poster Daddy had given me that said 'Dooley Dogs are No. 1.'"

Charles was nearly six when that Halloween photo was taken in 1966, and Vince Dooley's Dogs did, indeed, win the SEC championship that year, followed by a 24-9 victory over SMU in the Cotton Bowl that enabled Georgia to finish 10-1 and fourth in the final Associated Press poll.

The Seilers' two youngest children—daughters Bess and Sara—had similar experiences with the Ugas who lived at home when they were growing up. If they're not as closely associated with the mascots as Swann and Charles, it's because Bess and Sara both went to Brenau instead of UGA.

Uga I

Uga I's first road trip resulted in a 26-12 victory over North Carolina and a brief dognapping by a group of UNC fraternity boys.

NO HOUND DOG—Kenan Stadium's loudspeakers blared out "You Aint Nothing But A Hound Dog" Saturday but Uga, the University of Georgia's mascot, 'learned 'em.' He got the last growl when the Bulldogs chewed up North Carolina, 26-12. (Photo by Bill Prouty).

Early road trips were hazardous duty

Uga I's first road trip was to Chapel Hill, where, on October 13, 1956, the Dogs beat North Carolina 26-12. At that game, an AP photographer took a picture of Uga on the field with Coach Butts standing in the background. The photo (see above) won an Associated Press award, and it would remain the mascots' most famous on-field pose until Uga V nearly took a bite out of Auburn running back Robert Baker during Georgia's 56-49 four-overtime victory over the Tigers forty years later (see p. 108).

Uga I's trip to Chapel Hill back in '56 was not without incident, as a group of UNC fraternity boys made off with him briefly. Five years later, it happened again when Uga I was stolen from a car following the Auburn game in Athens. The Seilers spent a harrowing night looking for him with the help of the state patrol and local police. The incident ended on a positive note when Uga I turned up unharmed at a fraternity house on the Georgia Tech campus.

"The Tech boys said they had no idea how Uga got there," Sonny recalls. "But he was healthy and happy, which is all we cared about—and I think his captors realized that there's really no sport in taking Uga because he's so lovable. In those days, no charges were filed. Today, it would be a much different story."

To the Seiler children, Uga was—first and foremost—a pet. In this 1966 photo, Uga I poses with Sonny and five-year-old Charles, who's about to go trick-or-treating in his Georgia football uniform.

Trips to the vet school

The Southern climate is not the ideal environment for English bulldogs. Severe heat and humidity can cause skin problems and respiratory ailments, and the latter can be especially dangerous because English bulldogs have narrow air passages—which explains why there is a book about bulldogs called the *Flat-Faced Encyclopedia.* But thanks to expert care at the University of Georgia College of Veterinary Medicine, the Seilers' dogs have successfully avoided major respiratory problems.

Beginning with Uga I, each of the six mascots has undergone a procedure that is similar to a septoplasty in humans. It's performed under general anesthesia, with veterinary surgeons opening the dogs' nasal passages to give them more breathing room.

"English bulldogs have a structural condition that we call *brachycephalic*—which means, to put it bluntly, that they have a squashed face," says Dr. Bruce Hollett of the UGA College of Veterinary Science. "And because their skull is so short from front to back, they have a shortened air passage—which, fortunately, is easy to fix surgically."

For many years, these procedures were performed by UGA veterinary professor E.W. Causey, but Dr. Causey's expertise wasn't limited to the operating table.

"One morning in 1957, Uga I couldn't stand up," Sonny recalls. "He didn't seem to be in acute pain, but we had no idea what was wrong with him."

The Seilers took him to the vet school and waited anxiously while tests were done. "The vets manipulated his hind quarters," says Sonny, "and their diagnosis was that he might have a congenital problem in his spine. Our concern was that they might have to put him down."

Later that day, the Seilers got a telephone call from Uga's medical mainstay, Dr. Causey, who had heard about Uga's problem. He also knew how attached the Seilers were to Uga and how much the dog meant to the university.

"He told us that the diagnosis made by the other physicians was probably correct," Sonny recalls. "But he also told us that Uga's symptoms could be caused by something as harmless as . . . *acute constipation.*"

It isn't easy to give an English bulldog an enema—and Dr. Causey's exact instructions will not be repeated here. Suffice it to say that Sonny prevailed upon fraternity brother Fletcher Comer to help him work on Uga in the backyard of the Morningside Apartments in Athens. When the procedure was completed, Sonny and Fletcher held Uga still for as long as they could, then let him go.

"Things erupted like a volcano!" says Sonny. "Within a minute or two, Uga was up and running around the yard, tending to nature and delighted to be relieved of this terrible problem."

When it was time for Sonny to graduate from law school, he went to Coach Butts and reiterated his commitment to having Uga continue as the school mascot—even though he and Cecelia were moving to Savannah, where, after fulfilling his military commitment, Sonny would begin practicing law.

"I suggested to Coach Butts that he allow us to keep Uga, with the understanding that we would take him to all of Georgia's football games," says Sonny. "I held my breath for a couple seconds, and then Coach Butts, who had become very attached to Uga, smiled and said, 'Sounds like a good deal to me.'"

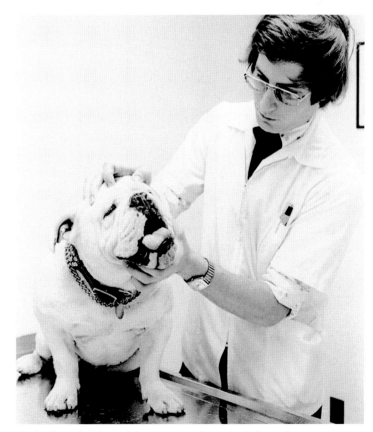

Uga I

The faculty and students of the University of Georgia College of Veterinary Medicine have been providing expert medical care for the mascots for nearly a half-century. The dogs' flat face—which veterinarians call brachycephallic—makes it hard for them to breathe, particularly when they get hot. To alleviate the problem, veterinary surgeons have widened the mascots' breathing passages.

Historic day at Grant Field

Travel was not very glamorous in the 1950s, particularly if you had an English bulldog in tow. And in '57, Georgia's football team was struggling through the third of what would become four consecutive sub-.500 seasons. Georgia had lost to arch-rival Georgia Tech eight years in a row, and, to make matters worse, the '57 Tech game was to be played at Grant Field in Atlanta.

Sonny needed to get both himself and Uga I from Savannah to Atlanta in time for the game—and he wasn't sure how he was going to do it. The Seilers' 1954 Chevrolet stationwagon was on its last legs, and flying was out of the question for two reasons: the cost was prohibitive for Sonny, and Eastern Airlines wouldn't carry Uga.

"Our only alternative," Sonny recalls, "was the Nancy Hanks, a Central of Georgia passenger train that ran between Savannah and Atlanta. A round-trip ticket was nine dollars. I could scare up the nine dollars for myself, but what was I going to do about Uga?"

In those days, railroads refused to carry pets. An exception clearly had to be made or Georgia would be without its mascot when it went into battle against its fiercest rival. Fortunately, Savannah attorney John Miller, a prominent Georgia alumnus who represented the railroad, worked a little behind-the-scenes magic that got Uga on board. Not in the passenger section, but in the mail car.

When Sonny and Uga I boarded the Nancy Hanks on Saturday morning, November 30, 1957, it was warm enough in Savannah for Sonny to opt for a summer suit. In his pocket, he carried a couple of turkey sandwiches Cecelia had made from Thanksgiving leftovers, plus two one-dollar bills.

"I tied Uga in the mail car and left him a bowl of water," Sonny recalls. "When it came time for lunch, most of the people went to the dining cars. But I didn't have enough money, so I went to the mail car and shared a turkey sandwich with Uga."

A fraternity brother picked up Sonny and Uga at the train station in Atlanta—where the temperature was thirty degrees colder than when Sonny left Savannah in his summer suit.

"The first half of the game was scoreless, I was freezing—and so was Uga," says Sonny, who left the sidelines at halftime in search of medicinal aid. Halfway up the stands, he spotted classmate Beryl Weiner, who gave him a swig of Jack Daniels that enabled him to survive until the game heated up.

Theron Sapp took care of that. In the third quarter, the Georgia halfback carried the ball on six consecutive plays down to the Tech 1-yard line. On fourth down, Sapp slammed through the right side of the line and into Georgia football history. The touchdown—the Dogs' first against Tech since '53—made the score 7-0.

The score held up, Sapp was known thereafter as "The Drought Breaker"—and Uga and Sonny were there to witness one of the most celebrated Georgia games of all-time.

And that was just the beginning.

ENTER GATE **24** NORTH STAND

SIDE LINE PASS

GEORGIA vs. GA. TECH

Sat., Nov. 30, 1957 - 2:00 P. M. EST

Grant Field

WORKING — Tax Free

N⁰ **40**

WELDON, WILLIAMS & LICK, FT. SMITH, ARK.

Pressure on Coach Butts caused by a string of losing games was dramatically lifted last November when his Bulldogs licked Tech, 7-0. Here, he is borne on the shoulders of his winning players as he shakes hands with Coach Bobby Dodd of Tech after the Georgia victory at Grant Field in Atlanta.

Sonny and Uga I took the train to Atlanta and saw history made at the 1957 game against Georgia Tech. Thanks to Theron Sapp's touchdown, Georgia snapped an eight-game losing streak to the Yellow Jackets. Wally Butts accepts congratulations from Tech coach Bobby Dodd.

Uga I

UNIVERSITY OF GEORGIA DEPARTMENT OF ATHLETICS
ATHENS, GEORGIA

ZEKE BRATKOWSKI
All-America T-QB 1953, N.C.A.A. passing leader 1952, punting champion 1953.

BOB McWHORTER
Georgia's First All-America Football Player, HB, 1913. Scored 61 TDs in Four Years.

GEORGE (Kid) WOODRUFF
Chairman G.S.E.F., Georgia Football Captain 1911, Head Coach 1923-27

WALLACE BUTTS
Georgia Athletic Director and Head Football Coach. SEC Champion 1942-46-48.

FRANK SINKWICH
All-America LHB at Georgia in 1941-42. Holds SEC Total Offense Record of 2,187 Yds.

CHARLES TRIPPI
All-America LHB at Georgia in 1946, All-America Short-Stop in 1946.

March 3, 1958

FORREST (Speck) TOWNS
Olympic High Hurdles Champion 1936. Held World Record 110-M. HH at 13.7 for 14 yrs.

JOHN CARSON
All-America End 1953. Quarter-finalist N.C.A.A. Golf 1951, 4-letter man.

Mr. Frank W. Seiler
208 East Bay Street
Savannah, Georgia

Dear Sonny:

    We wish to thank you for having your bulldog, "Uga" as our mascot at football games the past two years.

    "Uga" has grown into a truly handsome specimen of a bulldog and I know all Georgia alumni and friends are proud to have "Uga" as our official mascot.

    Please come to see us when you are in Athens.

    Kindest regards.

                    Sincerely,

                    Wallace Butts
                    Wallace Butts
                    Athletic Director

WB:sc

ZIPPY MOROCCO
All-SEC Guard at Georgia in 1953. Set SEC All-Time Scoring Record of 590 Pts.

SPURGEON CHANDLER
Georgia LHB 1929-30-31. All-Time New York Yankee Pitcher, Baseball's MVP in 1943.

BOB WALSTON
Georgia End 1948-49-50, Led Pro Scoring in 1954 (114 pts.) with Eagles.

REID PATTERSON
N.C.A.A. and National A.A.U. 100 yard Free Style Champion in 1953.

If you want to win you must pay the price
Wallace Butts

LINDSEY HOPKINS, III
Georgia Collegiate Tennis Singles and Doubles Champion 1956.

ARNOLD BLUM
S.E.C. Golf Champion 1942, Southern Amateur Champion 1951-1956.

When Coach Butts called Sonny into his office in '58, Sonny wondered if he'd done something to get himself fired. On the contrary, Butts wanted to be sure Sonny knew that the university wanted Uga I to continue as mascot even though Sonny would be leaving Athens to practice law in Savannah (see letter).

Uga I

Uga I

Over the years, the mascots have hobnobbed with lots of celebrities. One of Uga I's most memorable moments came in 1958, when he gave some "sugar" to Ty Cobb (center) on the sidelines of a Georgia football game. Cobb was the guest that day of UGA President O.C. Aderhold (left), but Uga came between the baseball immortal and college president and stole the show.

The mascots have entered only one dog show over the years, and Uga I might have fared better than third place at the Savannah Kennel Club's unbenched show in 1958—if he hadn't done something he shouldn't have in full view of the judges.

Uga's first bowl game is a victory!

Georgia didn't return to real prominence in football until 1959, when the Dogs won the Southeastern Conference championship in Athens with a nail-biting 14-13 victory over Auburn that was made possible by a fourth-down touchdown pass from quarterback Fran Tarkenton to end Bill Herron. Ironically, Vince Dooley was an assistant coach on the '59 Auburn team, and he remembers that day for more than just what happened on the field.

"I was stationed in the pressbox that day," says Dooley, an Auburn graduate who would become Georgia's head coach four years later, "and I remember how psyched the Georgia fans were prior to the game. I also remember seeing the cheerleaders waving this imitation War Eagle on a string and this all-white bulldog jumping up and grabbing at it with his mouth. That was my first look at Uga . . . and you could definitely say he was providing entertainment for the crowd."

The win over Auburn put Georgia in the Orange Bowl against Missouri. Uga I was there, too, but this time the train ride wasn't as problematic or the weather as cold. A large contingent of Savannah fans got reservations on the Atlantic Coastline train to Miami, and Uga was welcome—though still in the mail car.

"The major bowl games all had big parades back then," says Sonny. "The Orange Bowl

Scowling, Bug-Eyed Bulldog Goes Tiger-Hunting

parade was the night before the game, and one of our greatest thrills, to this very day, was seeing Uga I, in his red jersey, on the hood of a red Cadillac convertible leading the Redcoat Band and Georgia cheerleaders down Biscayne Boulevard."

That scene also made an impression on *Savannah Morning News* writer Tom Coffey, who thought he detected something in Uga's demeanor that translated to the Georgia team.

"The nonchalance of that reclining bulldog," Coffee would write years later, "seemed to convey the confidence of the football team."

The next day, Georgia beat Missouri 14-0 on a pair of Fran Tarkenton touchdown passes, and Uga had the first of what would become numerous bowl victories under his spiked collar.

SAVANNAH EVENING PRESS

GETTING ACCLIMATED—This is Uga, the University of Georgia football team's official mascot, and that's an orange bowl he's sitting beside. It's there to create an atmosphere for a journey that Uga will soon make. He's taking his first trip to a New Year's bowl game with the team, according to his owners, Mr. and Mrs. Frank Seiler. That's right, the Georgia Bulldogs' bulldog is going to Miami's Orange Bowl for the big Missouri game.

This bulldog balloon had a size advantage in the '59 Orange Bowl parade, but Uga I stole his thunder from his perch on the hood of a red Cadillac convertible that led the Redcoat Band down Biscayne Boulevard. Fran Tarkenton was the hero on the gridiron, throwing a pair of TD passes in a 14-0 Georgia victory over Missouri.

Uga I

Spiked collar and red jerseys

Uga I's first spiked collar came from Tuck's Shoe Shop in Athens. He and Uga II wore that same collar throughout their years of service; it is now on display in the mascot exhibit at the Butts-Mehre Heritage Hall on the UGA campus. Those early collars were made of brown leather, but nowadays Uga wears spiked collars made from red leather—size 24 and lined inside for comfort. The Seilers don't actually hook the leash to the spiked collar, which is mainly for looks. They use a soft choke collar for the leash because it is more comfortable for the dog and it works better in controlling him on the field.

Uga I's first spiked collar was made of brown leather by Tuck's Shoe Shop in Athens. Uga II wore the same collar, which was then replaced by the red leather version.

Cotton jerseys were a real problem in the early days at Sanford Stadium. Neither Uga I or Uga II had an air-conditioned doghouse where they could take refuge from the heat, as their successors have. As a result, they got really hot during Georgia's early-season games, where it's not unusual for the temperature to climb into the eighties or even nineties.

"Looking for any patch of shade they could find," says Cecelia, "Uga I and II would crawl under Sanford Stadium's famous hedges—snagging their cotton jerseys and creating holes that I was constantly having to mend."

The Seilers experimented with many different shirts and fabrics, all hand-tailored by Cecelia. Some of Uga's early outfits are also on display in the mascot exhibit at Butts-Mehre.

By the time Uga III had donned the spiked collar in the 1970s, textile manufacturers had developed new materials for use in football jerseys. These synthetic fibers worked much better than cotton—for both athletes and English bulldogs—because they were lighter in weight and also perforated to let the air in.

During Uga III's tenure, the Seilers became acquainted with Nonie Sutton and her husband, who were great Bulldog fans. Nonie owned and operated the Atlanta Sewing Company, and she was an expert seamstress.

The mascots' jerseys, which were originally handmade by Cecelia, have been created from a variety of materials with different textures, from stretch to ribbed to mesh.

Uga I

"At a Georgia game early in Uga III's tenure," Sonny recalls, "Nonie told me she could make him a shirt that would fit him better and look a lot better than the ones he'd been wearing. Little did she know that she was about to inherit a job that would be hers for decades!"

Nonie took to her Uga duties with a passion. She measured him with care and, true to her word, delivered a tailor-made jersey with a much better-looking "G."

"Thank God for Nonie!" says Cecelia. "Uga III looked really good in her jersey, and it lasted longer than the ones I had been fashioning at home."

When the Seilers made the switch to game-jersey fabric, the Georgia team's equipment ordered several yards of the same material that the players wore. Every time the spiked collar was passed to a new Uga, Nonie took new measurements, enabling her to tailor her jerseys to each dog's specifications.

"She's done such a good job," says Sonny, "that one sports writer referred to Uga as the best-dressed dog in America!"

When it came time for the 1997 premiere of the Warner Brothers movie, *Midnight in the Garden of Good and Evil,* Uga V was invited to the black-tie affair in Savannah (see p. 121). He had played the role of his father, Uga IV, in the movie, and, to mark the occasion, Nonie Sutton made Uga a black tuxedo, shirt, tie, and collar for his appearance on stage at the premiere. Uga VI later wore that same doggie formal attire to the gala opening of the University of Georgia's new alumni club in Atlanta (see p. 135).

When Uga V was mascot, Nonie Sutton passed her needle and thread to her daughter, Claudia Warthen, who is just as talented as her mother and also a devoted Georgia football fan.

"People call the athletic department all the time wanting to know where they can buy a jersey like Uga wears," says Sonny. "The answer is, they can't. These shirts are made specifically for the Georgia mascot and are not for sale. Nonie and Claudia have politely rejected many opportunities to make jerseys for other dogs and they're very proud to see Uga sporting their one-of-a-kind handiwork."

Uga I

Cecelia eventually passed her needle to Nonie Sutton, owner of the Atlanta Sewing Company, who created custom-made jerseys for the mascots. Her daughter, Claudia Warthen (at left), has now inherited that job, which has included creating a custom-made tuxedo for formal occasions like movie premieres and club openings.

It's not clear who's escorting whom in this 1962 photo of Uga I and Homecoming queen Emma Jo Jones. In those days, Sanford Stadium's famed hedges formed an archway at the east end of the field.

Football coach Johnny Griffin (center) is flanked by two of the most loyal and energetic University of Georgia supporters of all-time: at left, sports information director (and tennis coach extraordinaire) Dan Magill, who went looking for a new school mascot in 1956, and, at right, Sonny Seiler, who was only too happy to supply one.

Uga I

On February 22, 1964—the day the Coliseum was dedicated—cheerleaders escorted Uga I to the center of the court, where football coach Vince Dooley and Sonny Seiler accepted a portrait of the Georgia mascot painted by Savannah artist Mary Heriot.

Veterinary magic

In 1960, Uga I developed a serious health problem, this one requiring the help of people doctors.

Heartworms are a threat to all dogs—particularly those who live in the lowlands of Georgia, where mosquitoes are prevalent. In October 1960, Uga appeared very sluggish and slept excessively. He had lost weight and didn't want to go out, but the Seilers attributed his loss of appetite to hot weather. Dr. Ben Page, a graduate of UGA's College of Veterinary Medicine, diagnosed the problem as heartworms.

"It was a very traumatic diagnosis," says Sonny, "because the only accepted treatment for heartworms back then was to have the animal ingest an arsenic solution. It would kill the worms, but then you had to worry about the dog's system tolerating the arsenic and passing the worms."

Dr. Page happened to be familiar with a research project on heartworms that was being conducted at the Medical College of Georgia in Augusta. The doctor in charge of the research project was Charles R. Wallace, a graduate of the Auburn vet school, who was studying isolated cases of humans contracting heartworms. Dr. Page suggested that the Seilers prevail upon Dr. Wallace to examine Uga and treat him in Augusta.

"We didn't know Dr. Wallace," says Sonny. "But we did know Dr. Julian Quattlebaum Sr., who was one of Georgia's most prominent surgeons and also president of the UGA alumni society. *Nothing* was impossible for Dr. Quattlebaum, who called the president of MCG and made arrangements for Uga to be taken to Augusta."

On October 14, 1960, Dr. Wallace catheterized Uga I's heart, determined the extent of the damage, then treated the dog with the arsenic solution.

"Dr. Wallace said he thought we had detected the worms in time and that the procedure would be successful," Sonny recalls. "But he cautioned that the next forty-eight hours would determine whether Uga's system was strong enough to tolerate the arsenic and extinguish the worms."

It was touch and go for about a day, but Uga I not only survived but lived seven more years—and there was a bonus factor. A sufficient amount of arsenic remained in Uga I's system to prevent him from ever having a flea, tick, or heartworm problem again. This finding later helped veterinarians develop flea collars that are widely marketed for cats and dogs.

Gracing the cover of the October 24, 1964, football game program were Uga I with cheerleader Patty Tumlin, who married well-known Atlanta attorney—and UGA alumnus—Nick Chilivis.

Even a legend can't reign forever

By 1966, Uga I was in his tenth year of service. Prior to the football season, he showed signs of old age, and, while the vet school couldn't detect any specific ailments, his eyesight was failing and his energy was depleted. He could no longer run onto the field prior to games, and the Seilers decided that after a decade of loyal and meritorious service it was time for him to retire.

"I wrote a letter to athletic director Joel Eaves describing Uga I's symptoms and telling him that I didn't think he could make it through the season without difficulty," Sonny recalls. "Fortunately, Uga I's son, then just a year old, was waiting in the wings—full of vim and vigor."

Eaves thought it would be appropriate to have a retirement ceremony for Uga I just before kickoff at Georgia's Homecoming game against Kentucky on October 22, 1966. He planned the whole thing, and the crowd's reaction was spontaneous.

Prior to kickoff, the Redcoat Band lined the south side of the field as the P.A. announcer began a tribute to the retiring mascot. Uga I was already on the field, standing with four cheerleaders at the 50-yard line.

"As the announcer's voice filled the stadium," says Sonny, "my son Charles, who was just five years old, and I, accompanied by

a cadet colonel from the university's Air Force ROTC program, walked Uga II onto the field from the north sidelines. The crowd was already standing and applauding, and, ironically, just as the announcer told the crowd that Uga I was retiring and that this would be his last game, Georgia's longest-serving mascot, as if on cue, sat down on the field. Uga I had been a fur piece in his day, and he knew it was time to rest."

As one voice, 43,000 fans began chanting, "Damn Good Dog! Damn Good Dog! Damn Good Dog!" And they continued cheering for Uga I until both dogs had left the field and the Redcoats started playing. Moments later, when the Georgia team emerged from the dressing room, Uga II had his first Sanford Stadium romp as he and the cheerleaders led the team onto the field. Coach Eaves had the ceremonies filmed, and he later told the press that it was the most moving ceremony he had ever witnessed in sports.

The cheer "Damn Good Dog!" would be repeated many times over the years as the spiked collar was passed from one mascot to another.

Uga I waited patiently for the start of his retirement ceremony on October 22, 1966, and then—just as the P.A. announcer told the crowd that this would be his last game—the patriarch of the mascot line sat down on the field, as if he knew it was finally time to rest.

Father and son may look like mirror images of each other, but Uga I (right) had ten years and countless miles on Uga II as they met prior to the first changing of the collar ceremony.

Uga I

Uga I laid to rest at Sanford Stadium

On Thursday, November 9, 1967—two days before the Georgia-Florida game in Jacksonville—Uga I died peacefully while sleeping in the sun in the Seilers' backyard in Savannah.

"We had made the right decision to retire Uga I from active service the year before in Athens," says Sonny. "He died less than a month before his twelfth birthday. Although he had a number of ailments, he was never in pain. Old age just finally caught up with him."

Several weeks before, Sonny had conferred with Joel Eaves about a burial. Eaves felt Uga I should be buried within the confines of Sanford Stadium, and he made the arrangements through Boyd McWhorter, Georgia's faculty adviser for athletics. Tyus Butler, director of the alumni society, was also involved in the discussions. All parties agreed that no announcement of Uga's death would be made until after the burial.

On Friday, the day after Uga I's death, he was placed in a wooden coffin built by Bobby "Reds" Helmey at the Savannah Lumber Company.

"It was a simple pine box . . . painted red and black, of course," says Sonny.

Uga I's final trip to Athens was made by air, thanks to the Seilers' nextdoor neighbor, Charles Corbel, who was a pilot and owned his own plane. Sonny was met at the Athens airport by representatives of the UGA athletic department and taken immediately to the southeastern end of Sanford Stadium, where a grave had been prepared near the Georgia dressing room. Included in the gathering were Coach Eaves, Coach Dooley, Charles Corbel, and a small group of athletic personnel.

A few days later, a marble marker was placed over Uga I's grave.

By the weekend, news of Uga I's death had spread all over the state and the nation. Obituaries and editorials appeared in leading newspapers and hundreds of letters and cards poured in to the athletic department in Athens and to the Seiler family in Savannah, expressing appreciation for the life and service of a damn good dog.

Uga I

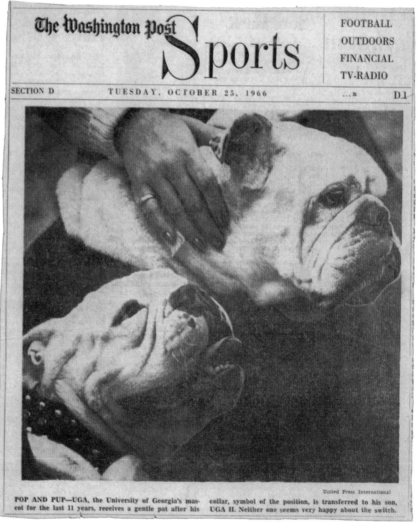

The Washington Post Sports

FOOTBALL
OUTDOORS
FINANCIAL
TV-RADIO

SECTION D TUESDAY, OCTOBER 25, 1966 ...R D1

POP AND PUP—UGA, the University of Georgia's mascot for the last 11 years, receives a gentle pat after his collar, symbol of the position, is transferred to his son, UGA II. Neither one seems very happy about the switch.

National news long before *Sports Illustrated* named his great-great grandson the country's No. 1 mascot—Uga I topped the *Washington Post* sports section on October 25, 1966. Actually, two Ugas did, as the *Post* ran a photo from Georgia's '66 Homecoming game, where—to a chorus of "Damn Good Dog!" from the stands—Uga I (above at right) passed his spiked collar to Uga II.

Uga II
1965–72

Born
January 22, 1965

AKC registered name
Ole Dan's Uga

Dates of service
October 22, 1966
to December 31, 1971

Football record
42-16-3

SEC titles
2
1966 (10-1)
1968 (8-1-2)

Bowl record
2-3

beat SMU 24-9
in '66 Cotton Bowl

lost to N.C. State 14-7
in '67 Liberty Bowl

lost to Arkansas 16-2
in '69 Sugar Bowl

lost to Nebraska 45-6
in '69 Sun Bowl

beat North Carolina 7-3
in '71 Gator Bowl

Died
April 28, 1972

Epitaph
"Not Bad for a Dog"

Uga II

Adding to Dad's Legacy

Swann Seiler was ten years old when Uga II came to live with her family. He was the first Uga she could really play with and keep up with, and she recalls their first meeting like it was yesterday.

"I can still remember going out to a farm in Millen, Georgia, to pick up Uga II . . . I had never been to a real farm before," says Swann. "It was a large litter and the puppies were lying on a flannel blanket in the backyard—but they were big enough to run around and nip at my shoes. There were some brindle-colored ones, which was the first time I'd ever seen a bulldog that wasn't all white. The puppies were jumping all over me, and I remember being a little scared—especially of the mama dog, who was being very protective of her puppies. My parents examined them all very carefully—and then

Uga II's tenure was the shortest of any of the mascots, but he was part of the resurgence of the Georgia football program under a young Vince Dooley.

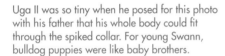

Uga II was so tiny when he posed for this photo with his father that his whole body could fit through the spiked collar. For young Swann, bulldog puppies were like baby brothers.

handed me an all-white one. He was so small he could fit in my coat pocket! I sat in the back seat of the car and held him all the way home to Savannah. I can still remember that new-puppy scent!"

Uga II had some big paw prints to fill. His father not only established the bulldog dynasty, he enjoyed what would stand as the longest tenure of any of Georgia's mascots—ten years. The spontaneous outburst of affection accorded Uga I as he stood at midfield for his retirement ceremony at the '66 Homecoming game is evidence of how much the patriarch of the mascot line was loved and admired.

But moments later, those boisterous cheers were transferred to the energetic heir who bounded onto the field ahead of the future SEC champions. In fact, if it hadn't been for a 7-6 defeat at Miami (Florida), Uga II's inaugural season might have produced a National Championship.

Uga II may have followed a legend, but he also had the good

fortune to begin his tenure as mascot just as Vince Dooley was coming into his own as a football coach. And though health problems prevented Uga II from serving more than six seasons—the shortest reign of all the mascots—he was around for a pair of SEC titles. He made five bowl-game appearances, and Georgia's record in football was a sparkling 42-16-3 (.713) during Uga II's reign.

Uga II brought a fresh burst of energy to the job—and Sanford Stadium crowds warmed to him immediately.

Uga II succeeded his father at a changing of the collar ceremony on October 22, 1966. With a Homecoming crowd looking on and Uga I waiting at midfield, Uga II was escorted onto the field by Sonny, who was accompanied by five-year-old Charles Seiler and a cadet colonel from UGA's Air Force ROTC program.

A first SEC title for Dooley and Uga

Having won the final five games of the '66 season—including a trifecta over Florida (27-10), Auburn (21-13), and Tech (23-14)—Georgia got a bid to play in the Cotton Bowl against SMU.

"It was a great trip for Georgia, for Uga II, and for all of our fans," Sonny recalls. "We traveled with the team to Dallas, where we rendezvoused with two of my good friends from Savannah, Billy Espy and Kirk Varnedoe. In those days, the Cotton Bowl parade was staged at the Dallas Fairgrounds, which surround the stadium. The morning before the game, the thermometer took a nosedive and the freezing temperatures prevented Uga II from taking his scheduled ride on a float. But he was proud to walk the entire parade route, with Ann DeLong and the rest of the Georgia cheerleaders handling his leash."

The Dogs beat SMU 24-9 on New Year's Eve, with future Clarke County state court judge Kent Lawrence's 74-yard touchdown run setting a UGA bowl-game record that still stands. The next day, Espy came up with tickets to the NFL Championship game in Dallas.

"In a twenty-four hour period," says Sonny, "I got to see Georgia win a bowl game and Bart Starr and the Packers beat the Cowboys," says Sonny. "It was a *wonderful* trip!"

Uga II

Sonny and Uga II at Sanford Stadium before the upper deck was added.

Uga II and Sonny were part of this post-game victory celebration as Georgia players hoist Vince Dooley onto their shoulders. Hired as head coach in 1964, Dooley won two SEC championships (1966, '68) during Uga II's tenure as mascot.

Dogs in the original dome

A year later, in game seven of the 1967 season, Georgia was back in Texas to do battle with another team from the Lone Star State. This time, the opponent was Houston and the venue was the Astrodome, which was billed as the "Eighth Wonder of the World" back then. Georgia had never played in a domed stadium; not many teams had.

Sonny and Uga II flew to Texas in a private plane with a group of Savannah fans, including Dr. Dicky Timms, Dr. Bucky Bergsteiner, Wiley Wasden, and Bill Metts.

"The flight was delightful and uneventful," Sonny recalls, "and Uga behaved better than his fellow passengers—but that's another story."

The Astrodome was an experience in itself. Uga was on the sidelines with the cheerleaders, doing his best to fire up a small red-and-black contingent, but Georgia lost a heartbreaker 15-14 in the closing minutes of the game.

"On the way back to Georgia, we stopped in New Orleans and had dinner at Arnaud's," Sonny recalls. "Uga II stayed at the airport, but to reward him for a long, tiring trip, we brought him a gourmet takeout bag of trout almondine!"

Never shy around pretty girls or photographers, Uga II poses with cheerleader Ann DeLong (left) and a member of the majorette corps (above).

Food, glorious food

Proper diet is important to the health of English bulldogs, and the Seilers have to be careful never to allow the mascots to exceed a certain weight; forty-five to fifty pounds was the ideal weight for Ugas I, II, III, and IV. Uga V could carry a little more weight, and Uga VI is the biggest of the lot at sixty pounds.

Uga I was raised on table scraps and a canned dog food named Twin Pet that was made from chicken by-products.

Uga II was raised on Jim Dandy, both canned and dry ration. But, in Sonny's estimation, canned dog food is not nearly as good for the dogs as dry food because it sticks to the dogs' teeth and can lead to early decay.

"To avoid those problems," says Sonny, "we get large beef femur bones from the butcher shop—usually the ball or knuckle part of the bone, which is about the size of a softball and mostly gristle. We boil these bones for an hour and, when they cool, give them to the dogs to chew. They don't splinter and there's no danger in letting Uga chew the bone right down to the nub. In the process, it cleans the dogs' teeth."

Ugas III, IV, and V all ate Jim Dandy Dog Ration, which came in fifty-pound bags. Ugas IV and V endorsed Jim Dandy, which worked out well because the athletic department got the royalties and the dogs got the food.

"We later changed Uga V to Hills Scientific Diet, which was much better for weight control and allergies," says Sonny. "It's also what we feed Uga VI, who eats his out of a personalized ceramic bowl given to him by Jack and Nancy Turner of Athens."

In 2001, the athletic department contracted with Hills for Uga VI to endorse Prescription Diet Z/D. The company published an attractive brochure with photos of Uga alone and with one of his UGA veterinarians, Dr. Bruce Hollett, of the UGA vet school. This brochure was sent out to 20,000 practicing veterinarians with Uga's endorsement of the product.

People often ask, "What is Uga's favorite food?"

"He will eat almost anything," says Cecelia. "He can lick the mayonnaise off a tomato and leave the tomato on the plate. He likes chicken and broiled fish, but without question his favorite food is roast turkey! All of these bulldogs love poultry, and on Thanksgiving Day—when they smell the turkey roasting—it drives them crazy! We make an exception on Thanksgiving and give the dogs a ration of turkey and gravy. But ordinarily, we're careful not to give Uga any table scraps or treats."

Uga IV's favorite meal was breakfast—and he was particularly interested on Saturday mornings in Athens when he could tell,

Uga VI with UGA veterinary professor Bruce Hollett, who advises the Seilers on genetic and reproductive matters regarding the mascots. This photo was included in an advertising flyer sent out by Hills Dog Food. In return for his endorsement of Hills, Uga VI gets free rations—and, as is the case with all of Uga's endorsements (see p. 104), the athletic association collects his appearance fee.

by the excitement level in the Seilers' room at the Georgia Center, that it was almost time to go to the stadium.

"We'd get an order of scrambled eggs and grits and bring it up to our room for Uga IV," says Sonny. "You can't imagine what an English bulldog looks like after eating a meal like that—he gets it all over himself! To avoid the mess, we put Uga IV in the bathtub with his grits and eggs and let him go to town. When he was done, we'd just turn on the water and wash him down right there in the tub. Over the years, you learn these tricks about bulldogs."

Uga IV was also the recipient of numerous doggie bags full of

Uga II

steak, courtesy of loyal Bulldogs Jim Ferguson, Billy Woodall, and their wives, whose habit was to leave the aromatic cuts of meat in a box outside the Seilers' room at the Georgia Center.

"One Friday night, Cecelia and I went to a party and stayed out later than usual," Sonny recalls. "In the meantime, Uga's benefactors had saved him a beautiful piece of medium-rare prime rib and left it in a white styrofoam box outside our door. Our son Charles, who was late getting to Athens that night, came up to the room before we got back. Seeing the box, he assumed the prime rib was for him and quickly made it disappear. None of us learned about the incident until the next morning—which explained why Uga was so interested in sniffing around the door. He was trying to figure out where his prime rib was!"

Weighing in at sixty pounds, Uga VI is easily the biggest and heaviest of the mascots. His ceramic bowl is easy to identify because it has his name on it, but Frank Lumpkin once mistook the contents of Uga V's metal bowl for human party mix.

Uga IV also got some great leftovers courtesy of the Seilers' good friend, Estelle Brown, who moved from Savannah to a beautiful historic home owned by her husband, Alan, in Washington, Georgia, less than an hour's drive from Athens. On football weekends, Estelle and Alan gave lavish brunches on Sunday mornings, and Uga IV always accompanied the Seilers, remaining in the car till his faithful friend Estelle would send out a tasty array of leftovers.

"On two occasions, I took Uga IV to Estelle's house on my way back to Savannah and Estelle fixed breakfast just for us," Sonny recalls. "Estelle was always very generous with Uga IV's

leftovers, but she refused to cook him more than one egg, never two. When he could manage, Uga IV always got two eggs at home—and, though that was seldom, he was of the opinion that two eggs was a meal and one just a snack. He would always look up at Estelle with a puzzled face wondering where the second egg was. Estelle never caught on and Uga never got but one egg."

When the topic of conversation turns to what Uga eats, the Seilers can't help recalling an incident that occurred at the Georgia Center in 1992.

Two of Georgia's most loyal alums, Richard Hecht and the late Frank Lumpkin, were instrumental in commissioning artist Wyndell Taylor's life-size bronze statue of Uga that stands in front of the mascots' graves in Sanford Stadium.

One Friday afternoon before a home game, Hecht and Lumpkin paid a visit to the Seilers' football weekend quarters at the Georgia Center to show Sonny and Cecelia photos of the prototype Taylor had made for the statue.

Uga II

"Cecelia had poured Uga V's dry dog food into a big aluminum bowl that the dogs have been using for years, and the bowl was sitting on a table in our room," Sonny recalls. "Cecelia and I were enjoying a beer, when Frank and Richard came in."

As the discussion over the statue became more and more animated, Lumpkin reached down and began helping himself to what looked to him like party mix—except it was Uga's dry dog food! He continued talking a mile a minute, and after each bite Cecelia would say, "Excuse me, Mr. Lumpkin . . . that's *dog food* you're eating." But Lumpkin, who was getting on in years and was hard of hearing, kept munching handful after handful of Uga's food. Cecelia finally began to get through to him, but the words still didn't register.

"Yeah, yeah, yeah . . . dog food, dog food, dog food," is all he would say.

"Finally, we just took the bowl away from him," says Cecelia. "When Frank realized what he'd been eating, he said, 'Oh hell, tastes pretty good to me . . . I guess I've eaten worse in my life.'"

GEORGIA | VS VMI

ATHENS, GA. SANFORD STADIUM OCTOBER 21, 1967 ONE DOLLAR

Uga II

Picture Day threatens Uga II's life

Before Picture Day got to be as popular as it is today (see Prologue), the official football team photograph was taken in late August at either Sanford Stadium or on the practice field next to the Coliseum. At this event in 1967, Uga II was dressed out in his jersey at Sanford Stadium just like the players. It was unbearably hot on the field—in the high nineties and not a breath of air.

A football program cover was being shot with Uga II surrounded by several players. It was late afternoon by the time the photo session finished—and, by that time, Uga II was almost finished himself.

"He wasn't used to the heat and I must confess to not checking him closely," Sonny recalls. "At the end of that prolonged posing session, Uga II suddenly dropped to the grass and rolled over—panting for his life."

Uga II had just finished posing for this game program cover in August 1967 when he collapsed with heat stroke. Sonny rushed him to the UGA vet school, where his temperature was measured at 107 degrees. An icy bath saved his life, but cost him his hearing later in life.

Sonny knew instinctively what to do. He picked up Uga II and ran to the men's restroom, holding the forty-five pound dog under a stream of cold water for a full five minutes. The cold shower revived Uga II, but he couldn't stand up. Fearing the worst, golf coach Dick Copas and Sonny rushed him to the UGA vet school, where the staff took his temperature. It was 107. To prevent him from having a stroke, the staff submerged Uga II in a tub of extremely cold water—which saved his life, but which would have repercussions later on.

Slowly but surely, Uga II's temperature came down. He was given intravenous solutions and kept overnight for observation. The next day, he was stable and allowed to go home. The Seilers learned a valuable lesson that day. From that point on, they were ultra-conscious of the heat, careful never to let the dogs get dehydrated or overheated. But some damage had already been done.

"As Uga II got older," says Sonny, "we realized that his hearing was impaired. During his last two years, he was totally deaf—but we never publicized it and both he and our family adapted to his handicap. He couldn't hear voice commands, but he could feel and recognize vibrations. By us stamping a foot, he would immediately look and come to us. In retrospect, veterinarians believe his unfortunate experience at Picture Day caused his deafness."

Staying cool while Dogs were hot on field

Like his father, Uga II had no cool place to go during a game except to take refuge under the trainers' table or burrow into the hedges—until Saturday, October 12, 1968, that is, when the "world's largest fireplug" was unveiled at the Ole Miss game.

"The red fireplug created a lot of interest among fans," says Sonny. "It was mounted on a thick steel platform with wheels, and it had a hinged door so Uga could crawl inside."

Initially, the fireplug was pulled onto the field by the cheerleaders as the Georgia team ran onto the field for the start of the game. Uga II would then emerge from inside the fireplug and run to his spot on the sidelines—to great applause. The fireplug would then be moved to the north sidelines near the cheerleaders' platform, where it would serve as a refuge for Uga for the remainder of the game.

Uga II's first fireplug was too heavy for the cheerleaders to manage very well, and it was later replaced by one made of fiberglass and mounted on a lighter platform with better tires. This is the same fireplug used for pre-game pageantry today, though the mascots no longer ride inside.

"Many people thought the first fireplug was air-conditioned . . . not exactly," says Sonny. "Bob Ennis, who makes all of Uga's beds, made him a round, plastic, zippered pillow that fit exactly into the

bottom of the fireplug. Before the game, Charles would fill the pillow with crushed ice. During breaks, Uga II would go inside the fireplug, plop down on the pillow, and cool off. It was a big improvement over the dogs hiding under the hedges in search of shade."

In recent years—beginning with Uga V—the mascots have, in fact, enjoyed air-conditioned comfort in their custom-made, air-conditioned doghouse, courtesy of Fred Hazlewood, a devoted fan and president of the Bahamian Bulldog Club in Nassau.

"It has a sure 'nuff air-conditioning unit that's plugged in prior to the game and kept at a temperature of fifty degrees," says Sonny. "It has a clear plastic door so that when Uga is inside, he can still see out and keep an eye on the game. For a breed of dog whose greatest enemy is the heat, the air-conditioned doghouse has been a godsend."

Uga II

ATHENS, GEORGIA, 30601, MONDAY, OCTOBER 14, 1968   TEN CENTS

'World's Largest Fireplug'

Long before there was an air-conditioned doghouse, Uga I and Uga II (shown here) had two ways to try to beat the heat at Sanford Stadium: hide under the trainers' table or burrow into the hedges. On October 12, 1968, Uga II got a reprieve when the Chevrolet Division of General Motors presented him with a fireplug-shaped shelter on wheels.

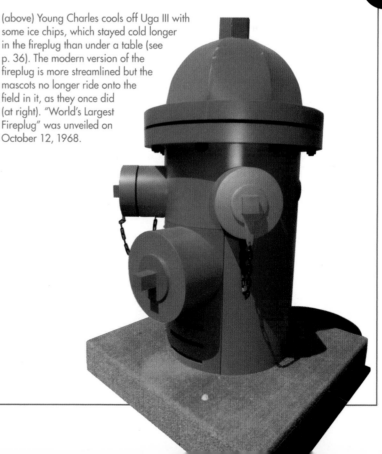

(above) Young Charles cools off Uga III with some ice chips, which stayed cold longer in the fireplug than under a table (see p. 36). The modern version of the fireplug is more streamlined but the mascots no longer ride onto the field in it, as they once did (at right). "World's Largest Fireplug" was unveiled on October 12, 1968.

37

Uga V was the first mascot afforded the luxury of an air-conditioned doghouse, courtesy of Fred Hazlewood, a devoted Georgia fan and president of the Bahamian Bulldog Club in Nassau (shown here with Uga VI and Hairy Dawg).

Uga II

The 1968 team had reason to be ecstatic after beating Auburn 17-3 to clinch the conference title. The locker room celebrants included Sonny, Charles, and Uga II, plus—can you spot them?—Billy Payne, Kent Lawrence, and Bill Stanfill.

SEC Champs 1968 - Coach
Brother Seiler, Age 8
Dressing Room Celebration
Cliff Hare Stadium
Georgia 17 - Auburn 3
Saturday, Nov. 16, 1968

Mike Cavan and UGA II
Dressing Room
Cliff Hare Stadium
Georgia 17 - Auburn 3
Saturday, Nov. 16, 1968

Future Georgia assistant coach Mike Cavan felt so good after beating Auburn to win the '68 SEC championship that he had to give Uga II a squeeze.

In the old days, when the Seiler kids were young, the entire family would pile into a red station wagon on Friday afternoons and set sail for Athens. With three people in front and three in back, there was just enough room for Uga II's kennel in the cargo area. Luggage? "We packed light," says Cecelia.

Uga II

Georgia Center: Uga's home away from home

Located across Carlton Street from Stegeman Coliseum on the UGA campus, the Georgia Center for Continuing Education is the mascots' home away from home.

"We started staying there with Uga I in 1958, when the standard room rate was $14.50 a night," says Sonny. "In those days, the university had a policy preventing pets from staying in the Georgia Center—a rule that even included its school mascot, who wasn't welcome in the only on-campus hotel."

The anti-pet policy was a major aggravation for the Seilers, who refused to even consider putting the school mascot in a kennel when they brought him to Athens. They got around the rule by waiting until after dark to slip Uga up the fire escape and into their small two-room suite. The process was reversed at daybreak, when Uga was returned to the Seilers' car, as though he'd slept there all night.

The Seilers' two-room suite was sealed off from the rest of the floor by a hallway door, making it an ideal place to isolate children and their canine contraband.

"Cecelia and I would feed the children early and put them to bed," says Sonny, "Then we'd go out on the town and return after dinner, knowing they were safe at the Georgia Center."

Safe, yes. But unbeknownst to mom and dad, the Seiler kids looked upon the Georgia Center as their own private amusement park. As soon as Sonny and Cecelia left for dinner, Swann and her two little brothers—Charles and the reigning Uga—would embark on an indoor night on the town.

"The Georgia Center was considered a state-of-the-art conference facility," says Swann. "With a maze of corridors, meeting rooms, commons areas, and classrooms, it was just perfect for playing hide-and-seek!"

Quiet until they had exited their hotel floor, Swann, Charles, and Uga were as exuberant as kids on a playground once they had made their way into the Georgia Center's dimly-lit conference areas, which weren't used at night.

"Charles and I would hide and Uga would come find us!" says Swann in a tone of voice that suggests she would still consider it fun lo these many years later. "You knew when he was getting close because you could hear his paws pounding along the corridor and the collar around his neck jangling. We screamed and yelled and had the time of our lives! But to my knowledge, we never disturbed anyone—and no one ever found out."

Until they told their parents—years later, that is, when Swann and Charles were adults themselves and well past the point of getting into trouble.

The Seilers now drive a shiny, red sport utility vehicle—the seventeenth station wagon or SUV they've transported the mascots in over the years. And when they reach their home away from home—the Georgia Center for Continuing Education—the Seilers are grateful to find a parking place reserved for Uga, which makes it easier for them to get him in and out of the facility on football weekends.

Uga II

As Uga's popularity grew, so did the university's appreciation for his comfort and well-being. In the late 1970s, at the urging of UGA president Fred Davison, the Georgia Center's policy was changed, enabling the school mascot—Uga III by that time—to stay there as a recognized guest, coming and going through the front door instead of the fire escape.

"In recent years," says Sonny, "wonderful people like Jeannie Epps and Pat Salum have made the mascots' stays at the Georgia Center a lot easier."

Uga attracts a great deal of attention on game day, beginning in the Georgia Center lobby, where crowds gather just to catch a glimpse of him emerging from the elevator. They snap photos of him in his red game-day jersey, then follow him out to the Seilers' red sport utility vehicle, which is always parked in a reserved parking space in the Georgia Center's circular driveway on Carlton Street.

UGA president Charles Knapp was so enamored with the mascots and so mindful of their importance to the university that he and his wife Lyn extended a special invitation for Uga IV to attend a Presidents Club reception at their house on the first home football weekend of Knapp's administration in 1987. Until President Fred Davison changed the policy in the late 1970s, the Seilers had to sneak Uga up the fire escape at night and return him to their car first thing next morning.

The "visiting coach from Shanghai Tech"

When you travel with the Georgia mascot, you meet all kinds of interesting people. Take Jack Peng, for example. He came to the University of Georgia to get his Ph.D. in physics at about the same time Coach Dooley was assembling his first coaching staff in 1964.

"Jack tutored players in science courses, rarely missed a practice, and showed up on the sidelines for every home game," says Sonny. "He always wore a smile, and he had an amazing knowledge of football."

Uga II and Sonny met Peng at the '68 Georgia-Tennessee game in Knoxville, where the Vols tied the eventual SEC champion Bulldogs 17-17 on a controversial play as time expired.

"We all took an instant liking to Jack," says Sonny, "and from that day until he left Athens ten years later he would always ride to and from the game in our red station wagon."

Georgia's vaunted defensive coordinator, Erk Russell, was so fond of Peng that he dubbed him "the visiting coach from Shanghai Tech." Erk introduced him to the team that way, and, to Peng's delight, the nickname stuck.

"Jack Peng considers himself an expert in Asian cuisine, and his egg rolls are pretty good," says Sonny. "But Jack has also been known to have a cocktail or two while cooking, and it's not unusual for him to end up with more flour on himself and the kitchen floor than on the eggs rolls!"

One April, when they were in Augusta at the Masters golf tournament, Cecelia and Sonny and their friend Harry Middleton went to their car for a sandwich and a beer. Harry had the tailgate open when he overheard a passing fan say to his companion, "There's that red station wagon . . . this is the first time I've seen that damn car that it didn't have a bulldog and a Chinaman in it."

Uga is amazing . . . but he cannot walk on water

During the late 1960s and early 1970s, when Georgia played at Auburn, the Seilers would spend the weekend with Jack and Ann Swertfeger on a farm owned by Mr. and Mrs. Paul Daniel

---

[THEY SAID IT]

"IT CAN BE ARGUED that there is no more appealingly unhandsome a canine in all of dogdom today than the bulldog. A wrinkled dog of brute strength, unparalleled courage and bullheaded stubbornness, the bulldog's creased face can break into a doggie grin that will melt any disbeliever's heart. If you want a loyal, affectionate dog brimming with charm and personality, the bulldog may be the breed for you."

—Kim D.R. Dearth,
Dog World magazine

---

at Camp Hill, Alabama. The Auburn crowd, led by Jack and Ann, always outnumbered the Georgia contingent. But the Seilers and their friends Oscar and Dot Wansley still felt like they held the balance of power because they had Uga on their side—first II and later III.

"There were several ponds on the property," says Sonny, "and on Friday afternoons we would all go down to the one behind the house to catch the evening's supply of catfish. One Friday, we arrived late. It was almost dark, but still light enough to see."

Uga II was a city dog who knew little about the country—and even less about water. The late afternoon shadows cast an eerie glow across the surface of the pond.

"To Uga II, it must have looked liked a paved parking lot," says Sonny, "because as soon as we let him out of the car he made a mad dash down the hill to where Jack and the others were fishing. Instead of stopping at the edge of the pond, he just kept right on going! You should have seen the look on his face when he found himself over his head in the cold water—with everyone on the bank, his owners included, laughing hysterically. Uga found out fast, he's no Bear Bryant!"

All kidding aside, bulldogs don't do well in water. They like water, but they don't do well in it.

"All of the mascots have had access to our cottage at Tybee Beach," says Sonny. "Before it became unlawful to have a dog on the beach, they liked to go down and splash around in the surf—with the exception of Uga VI, who doesn't even like to walk in soft sand. We also have a boat named *Silver Britches,* and the dogs delight in riding in it late in the afternoon when it's cool.

"But we have to watch them carefully because, although bulldogs can swim, they can't guide themselves to safety. If they fall overboard—or slip into a swimming pool—they run the risk of drowning. Uga III's mother, Georgie Gal, who was owned by Andy and Peggy Hill of Lavonia, Georgia, met her demise when she accidentally fell in the family swimming pool and drowned."

When it came time to leave for the Auburn game on that

Uga II

Saturday morning in Camp Hill, Jack Swertfeger insisted on driving the red station wagon with Uga in the back. That was fine with the Seilers because Jack knew all the shortcuts to the stadium. But it did look funny to Auburn fans to see Jack—decked out in Auburn colors from head to toe—chauffeuring the Georgia mascot!

"One year when Jack was driving," says Sonny, "an Alabama state patrolman radioed ahead that an Auburn fan had apparently stolen the Georgia mascot car and to be on the lookout!"

Mascots travel in style

All of the mascots have traveled in red station wagons like the ones Jack Peng rode in, or, in recent years, in red sport utility vehicles. Over the years, the Seilers have owned seventeen of these vehicles. Recently, they switched to a red Ford Expedition for Uga VI because they needed a bigger vehicle for a bigger dog.

"We've never asked for the use of a dealer car because we don't want to over-commercialize these dogs," says Sonny. "But Uga does have his own official license plate—courtesy of Bobby Lenihan, a friend and loyal Georgia supporter, who reserves these plates for the dogs."

Every time the State of Georgia changes license plates, Uga's name is reserved for the new one. In addition, the state provides an ornamental tag for the front of the car, which reads: University of Georgia Mascot.

"This tag is a great help in negotiating traffic to and from a game," says Sonny. "Our fans recognize the vehicle and give us the right of way for safe passage."

When traveling by air, the Georgia team always takes a charter flight on Delta Airlines. Over the years, Delta has given each of the mascots a large travel kennel, where the dogs can rest comfortably on the way to Athens for home games, to the Atlanta airport for away trips, and in hotel rooms. This practice began during Uga II's tenure, when the kennels were square and wooden. Later, high-impact plastic kennels replaced the wooden ones.

Bobby Lenihan, Georgia's assistant state revenue commissioner, reserves a vanity plate for the Seilers' SUV every year, plus an ornamental tag for the front of the SUV.

Uga II

"On charter flights, Delta regulations allow Uga to ride in the cabin with the team," says Sonny. "He usually stays in the back of the plane, where the flight attendants can't resist giving him milk and snacks. But he is just as comfortable traveling in his kennel in the pressurized baggage compartment when we have to take a commercial flight."

For the most part, flying with Uga is relatively uneventful. But it requires a great deal of vigilance on the Seilers' part.

"I remember going to the 1976 Cotton Bowl," says Sonny, "when, just as we were about to take off, I happened to look out the window and see—to my horror—Uga III in his red kennel being loaded into the belly of the plane next to ours! If we hadn't caught the mistake, Uga would have ended up in Chicago and we would have been in Dallas."

When Uga travels by car or in the baggage compartment of a plane, he enjoys the comfort and security of his Delta Airlines carrier. But on team charters (see Uga IV with Delta's stewardess Susan Powell and charter hostess Judy Belcher and Uga V with Georgia football coach Ray Goff and sideline reporter Loran Smith), he rides in the cabin—where he's spoiled rotten by flight crews.

43

No-name subs: Bugga Lou and Knute

During the summer of 1971, Uga II began to lose weight and energy. The Seilers changed his diet and began taking him to the vet. He rallied sufficiently to be taken to the '71 season opener, a 56-25 victory over Oregon State in Athens, but he wouldn't run onto the field before the game. By mid-season, he had been diagnosed with a form of leukemia.

His health was such a concern that a substitute mascot needed to be found for both the South Carolina and Florida games. Fortunately, the Seilers had a worthy stand-in waiting in the wings, an English bulldog named Bugga Lou who was noteworthy for two reasons:

She was female, and, by country of origin, a genuine *English* bulldog.

"Bugga Lou was given to us by some people who had brought her from England but could no longer care for the dog in Savannah," Sonny recalls. "She wasn't even white; she was brown and white, but we had to press her into service when Uga II got sick. And she won both games!"

No formal announcement was made about the change, and, surprisingly enough, the news media was clueless to the late-season switch. The Jacksonville paper published a photo of Bugga Lou on the sidelines at the Florida game with a headline above the photo that read:

"He's Uga, And He Spurred Bulldogs to a Win."

Uga II was able to return for the final two games of the '71 season and for Georgia's trip to the Gator Bowl. (Bugga Lou died March 5, 1977, and is buried at the Seilers' cottage at Tybee Beach.)

Uga II had sired an all-white male puppy named Argos, who was named for Odysseus' dog in Homer's *The Odyssey*.

". . . and Odysseus returned. There lay the dog, Argos, full of vermin. Yet even now, when he was ware of Odysseus standing by, he wagged his tail and dropped both ears but near to his master, he had not now the strength to draw. But Odysseus looked aside and wiped away a tear. . . ."

Thinking Argos wouldn't be needed for mascot duty, the Seilers gave him to Sonny's sister, Ann Robertson, who lives in Maryland.

"Ann, in her infinite wisdom, changed his name from Argos to

The Seilers never thought that Knute, an all-white son of Uga II, would need to serve as mascot—so they gave him to Sonny's sister, who lived in Maryland. But when Uga II died of leukemia, Knute had to be pressed into service for one game—the 1972 season opener—before young Uga III was old enough to take the field.

Knute—but we ended up needing him," says Sonny. "After Uga II's death, and before Uga III was big enough to serve, we used Knute for the '72 home opener in Athens against Baylor—and he was great. We quietly returned him to Ann as soon as Uga III was coronated at the N.C. State game in Athens on September 30, 1972."

Uga II becomes seriously ill

Uga II managed to finish the '71 season, including a 28-24 victory over Georgia Tech in Atlanta and a 7-3 win over North Carolina in the Gator Bowl on New Year's Eve in Jacksonville. The Gator Bowl win enabled the '71 team—which posted four shutouts en route to an 11-1 record—to finish the season ranked No. 7 in the final AP poll.

But by the spring of 1972, Uga's leukemia was compounded by kidney problems. Sonny was serving as president of the State Bar of Georgia at the time, and during the last week in April he was asked to speak at the annual meeting of the Georgia Legal Secretaries Association in Atlanta. After he left Savannah, Uga II took a turn for the worst and a friend, Dan Jardine, had to drive him back to the UGA vet school. It would be his final trip to Athens.

Uga II

Uga II died at the UGA vet school on the last Friday of the month—before Sonny could even get to Athens. Cecelia called his longtime secretary, Marie Storrs, at the legal secretaries meeting in Atlanta and asked her to give him the bad news. Early Saturday morning, Marie drove Sonny to Athens for Uga's burial.

"We went directly to Sanford Stadium, where the grave had already been prepared next to his father's," Sonny recalls. "No announcement had been made of Uga II's death, and, by design, only a handful of people showed up for the internment. Coach Eaves was there. So was Coach Dooley and Dan Magill. As I drove back to Savannah, I did so with a heavy heart. I had just said goodbye to another member of our family."

By Sunday, papers all over the country carried the news of Uga II's death and burial. In the weeks to come, the Seilers received many kind letters, cards, and calls from the faithful.

Uga II's Christmas ornaments

Over the years, the mascots have received countless gifts: brushes, bed cushions, collars, leashes—just about anything a dog could use. Hotels often send a basket of treats to Uga's room as soon as the Seilers check in. The Hazlewoods of the Bahamas sent Uga a real straw hat that actually fit him! It still hangs in the Seilers' den.

The most frequent gift is food, which the Seilers accept graciously—but rarely does Uga get a taste. The Seilers keep the mascots on a very controlled diet.

"The most meaningful gift Uga ever received," says Sonny, "was a series of homemade Christmas tree ornaments—beautiful red satin balls with the mascot's name and the year in black—which were sent every year by Helen Fukushima of Athens. Helen's gifts started with Uga II and continued for more than twenty years. One year, we realized that Helen's ornament didn't arrive. The next year, it didn't either. And then, sadly, we learned that Uga's faithful friend, Helen, had passed away."

Georgia Alumni Record

November 1971

THIS ISSUE: UGA II AND FRIEND, THEIR STORY

Uga II was suffering from leukemia when he and Sonny posed for the cover of the November 1971 *Georgia Alumni Record.*

Tribute to Uga II

A few months after Uga II's death, David C. Barrow Jr.,
a prominent Savannah attorney, penned a beautiful tribute to Uga II:

Uga II

No mascots ever known to man,
With any team in this great land,
Have been as faithful, good and true,
As Georgia's Ugas One and Two.

This tribute is to Uga Two
Whose years on earth were far too few,
Who now we know, tho much in pain,
Was with his master shine or rain;

And every week morale was raised,
By Uga who was loudly praised
By every student, every teacher,
Hailing this courageous creature.

Could he have made a last request
I'm sure he'd seek eternal rest
At Sanford Field, by grace of God,
Where he sleeps now beneath the Sod.

—David C. Barrow Jr.
Savannah, Georgia, June 1972

UGA II

GEORGIA MASCOT
1966-1972
TWO S.E.C. CHAMPIONSHIPS
FIVE BOWL TEAMS
"NOT BAD FOR A DOG"

Uga III
1971–81

Born
October 9, 1971

AKC registered name
Seiler's Uga Three

Dates of service
September 30, 1972
to September 5, 1981

Football record
70-31-2

SEC titles
2
1976 (10-2)
1980 (12-0)

Bowl record
2-4
beat Maryland 17-16
in '73 Peach Bowl

lost to Miami (O.) 21-10
in '74 Tangerine Bowl

lost to Arkansas 31-10
in '76 Cotton Bowl

lost to Pittsburgh 27-3
in '77 Sugar Bowl

lost to Stanford 25-22
in '78 Bluebonnet Bowl

beat Notre Dame 17-10
in '81 Sugar Bowl

National
Championships
1
1980

Died
September 22, 1981

Epitaph
"How 'Bout This Dog"

Uga III

National Championship Dog!

With a head and chest that are disproportionately large compared to the rest of their body—owing to judging standards that dictate that the circumference of the head be at least equal to the height at the shoulder—bulldogs are the middle linebackers of the canine world. And as football fans got more and more familiar with him during his nine-year tenure, Uga III came to symbolize the strength, grit, and determination that Georgia's football teams have traditionally displayed on the gridiron.

During Uga III's tenure as mascot, the "television era" brought unprecedented popularity to college football. From 1972-80, Georgia appeared on national TV a dozen times, regional TV nine times—and during those telecasts the cameras just naturally

During Uga III's nine-year reign, the "television era" brought unprecedented popularity to college football, to the Georgia program, and to the mascots.

Uga III

With a head and chest that are disproportionately large compared to the rest of their body, bulldogs are the middle linebackers of the canine world.

gravitated to Uga III, whose increased visibility and popularity made him one of the icons of college football. He would be on duty for a period of unparalleled success for the Georgia football team, culminating in the Bulldogs' greatest season of all-time.

Uga II had died in the spring of 1972, but his personality and showmanship had obviously rubbed off on his son while the two dogs were sharing the Seilers' backyard in Savannah. By the fall of 1972, Uga III—though scarcely more than a pup—was ready for the spiked collar. He was introduced to the Sanford Stadium crowd at Georgia's second home game against North Carolina State on September 30, 1972.

"Coach Eaves had carefully planned Uga III's introduction," says Sonny. "Prior to kickoff, the public address announcer summarized Uga II's career, while my son Charles, who was eleven at the time, walked Uga III around the perimeter of the stadium, accompanied by the cheerleaders. The Redcoat band had formed a double line on the field, and as the announcer introduced Uga III, Charles proudly walked him onto the field and then back to the hedges as the band played 'Hail to Georgia Down in Dixie.' Moments later, Charles led Uga III on his first romp onto the Sanford Stadium turf with the cheerleaders and players right behind them."

An exemplary tour of duty awaited Uga III. His father's last team went 11-1 and finished the '71 season ranked No. 7 in the country. But in Uga III's nine seasons as mascot, Georgia finished in the top 20 seven times.

Athletic director Joel Eaves had carefully planned Uga III's introduction to the Sanford Stadium crowd on September 30, 1972. At the appointed time, eleven-year-old Charles Seiler led the new mascot onto the field for the first time.

When Georgia Tech graduate Sam Nunn was campaigning for the U.S. Senate in 1972, he made a special trip to Sanford Stadium in order to be photographed with Uga III. The signature on this photo, taken with cheerleader Janet Ross, says, "This brings back memories of the 1972 election and played a big role in my win. Thanks! Sam"

The road to Athens

As far as the Seilers are concerned, there are only two ways to get from Savannah to Athens for a football weekend—the old-fashioned, two-lane route they used to take through small towns like Bloomingdale, Guyton, and Egypt, and the new four-lane route they switched to once I-16 opened.

"If you've got Uga with you, you can't make it in less than four hours because you've got to stop a couple of times to walk him," says Cecelia, who always does the driving while Sonny either reads or sleeps. In the course of forty-five years, Cecelia and Sonny have driven to Athens more times than some people have gone to their neighborhood grocery. But Cecelia says she doesn't mind. "You can count the barbecue places, keep an eye peeled for the reindeer farm near Sandersville, or think about what you want for breakfast," she says. "Plus, we love Athens so much, we'd probably do it even if it were an eight-hour drive!"

The Seiler kids grew up in Savannah, but spent so much time in Athens—and in the car going to and coming from—that they think of the Classic City as their second home.

"Daddy has become a very successful lawyer," says Swann. "But in the early days, we couldn't afford motel rooms for six people and a dog for two nights—so we'd stay in Savannah on Friday night, then leave for Athens at the crack of dawn Saturday morning."

Rousted out of bed before anyone else in their neighborhood was awake, the Seiler kids slept like rocks till it was time for breakfast. But they were awake from then on, which made every trip an adventure. The Seilers drove a station wagon because of Uga. But with four kids, two adults, and a mascot along for the ride—plus luggage and weekend refreshments and supplies—there wasn't a cubic inch to spare. In the early days, Uga didn't have a kennel; he stayed in the cargo area with the luggage. At least that was the plan. But if one of the kids moved a muscle to look out the window or put away a game, Uga would take advantage of the opening.

"He'd climb into the back seat and steal my space and my blanket," Swann recalls. "And when you're a little kid, it's not that easy to move a fifty-pound dog!"

The Seiler kids grew up in Savannah, but spent so much time in Athens that they came to think of it as their second home. In those days, the Seilers parked their station wagon in the Coliseum parking lot, and the girls—oldest sister Swann (above) and her younger sisters Sara and Bess (below)—liked to sit on the roof with Uga III.

Uga III

"It's hard to remember a trip where Uga wasn't with us," says Charles.

Uga III

"We have four youngsters and they have tried the dogs' temper numerous times, but none of the dogs has so much as growled at them."

Sonny Seiler

In the old days, when Uga I and II wore the spiked collar, the Paradise Restaurant was the Seilers' breakfast destination, not just for the bacon and eggs but because Uga needed a drink and a walk by then.

"Louisville was next," says Sonny. "We'd stop at Al Thomas' service station to fill up with gas, walk Uga again, and talk with our dear friend Al and his family. When we first stopped there, 'young Al' was just a boy, and we watched him grow up over the years—along with Tina, the Thomases' three-legged dog."

Recommended by friends Irv and Marey Wofford, the Seilers got hooked on Hill's Barbecue on the outskirts of Louisville. Or at least some of the Seilers did. Sonny wasn't a fan. But if he was trying a case in Atlanta and meeting the family in Athens, the barbecue shack was a regular mother-daughter ritual for Cecelia and Swann.

"We would eat our barbecue sandwiches en route—and praise our good luck at not having Daddy along because he didn't like the way the place looked," says Swann. "On one of Uga V's first trips to Athens, he got a whiff of our barbecue and started howling like the Hound of the Baskervilles. He sounded so forlorn that Mama finally broke her 'no-snack rules' and bought him a fast food burger to shut him up."

From Louisville, the Seilers would continue on the back roads to Mitchell and then cross the bridge at Shoals, Georgia, which spans the headwaters of the Ogeechee River.

"By the time we got to Sparta, first passing by the famous House of the Thirteen Sisters, it was time for the highlight of the trip—who could be the first to spot the Iron Horse!" says Swann. "From Sparta, we'd take Highway 15 through Greensboro, and eventually the Iron Horse would appear in farmer Jack Curtis' pasture on the right side of the car. I always wanted to get out of the car and touch the Iron Horse, but Daddy claimed a mean bull guarded that pasture."

"He did!" says Sonny.

Watkinsville was next, and then finally the Seilers' home away from home—the Georgia Center for Continuing Education, in the heart of the University of Georgia campus.

"The new way—once I-16 opened—is a little shorter, though not nearly as interesting," says Sonny. "We stop in Metter to eat at Jo Max Barbecue, then take the Adrian/Soperton exit to Highway 15 through Wrightsville—home of Herschel Walker. Then it's on to Tennille—home of Robert and Terrence Edwards—and then Sandersville, followed by Sparta, Greensboro, and Athens."

When Georgia swimming coach Jack Bauerle first asked the Seilers to bring Uga III around to meet recruits, the Swim Dogs weren't very good and Bauerle was looking to divert attention from the school's outdated pool at Stegeman Hall—where Sonny had sold tickets as a college student. It took awhile but the formula worked, as Uga V was present at the meet in 1999 when the Georgia men upset No. 1-ranked Texas.

Uga III

Uga's fame extends north of Mason-Dixon line

Jack Bauerle grew up in Philadelphia, and his best sport was always swimming. But even as a kid, he was an avid Georgia football fan. "I loved Erk Russell's Junkyard Dog defenses," says Bauerle, who came to Georgia both to swim and to see Jake Scott and Bill Stanfill play in person.

Bauerle swam for Georgia from 1971–75, and he never missed a home football game unless he had a meet. But when he went home for holidays or in the summer, his Philly friends weren't content to just talk football and swimming.

"They'd tell me, 'Wow, what a great mascot you guys have!'" says Bauerle, "and they'd all want to know, 'What's Uga really like?'"

Bauerle was captain of the Georgia swimming team from 1974–75, in the midst of Uga III's tenure as mascot. When he took over as men's swimming coach in 1979, Bauerle began calling on Uga and Sonny, a swimming letterman himself, to provide little perks for recruits.

"What's so impressive about Sonny and the way he handles Uga," says Bauerle, "is that he'll do anything he can to help the University of Georgia. When he first started bringing Uga around to meet recruits, we weren't very good. But Uga gave us something special to show kids when we didn't want them looking at old Stegeman pool! And he was there—Uga V, I guess it was by then—when the Georgia men upset No. 1-ranked Texas in 1999."

Bauerle now coaches both the men's and women's swim teams at Georgia, and he was an assistant coach at the 2000 Olympic Games in Sydney. The Lady Swim Dogs won three consecutive NCAA championships (1999–2001) under his tutelage, and Uga has contributed to the swim team's success by making regular appearances at Homecoming weekend activities for swimming alumni and recruits.

"Recruits get so excited meeting Uga!" says Bauerle. "He's such an endearing . . . well, I started to say *animal,* but he's really surpassed that. Uga reminds me of our team. We're not always blessed with the most *talent*—or, in his case, I guess you could say *looks*—but we're *fierce competitors.*"

College did little to distract Swann from remaining close to Uga III. She helped care for him at the 1976 Cotton Bowl, and he sometimes stayed at her Athens apartment when he had appointments at the vet school.

Uga III

Pink pooch

In 1977, Uga III's oldest sister Swann was a student at UGA, majoring in journalism/public relations, and when Uga III needed treatment at the vet school it was convenient for him to stay at Swann's apartment.

"In those days, we were still making Uga's jerseys out of a child's red T-shirt," says Cecelia, "so we asked Swann to find a size 8 shirt for Uga to wear at the next game."

So Swann went to Gibson's department store and, with the help of good friend and future Emmy Award winner Deborah Norville, she picked out what she thought was an ideal shirt for Uga. Cecelia transformed it into a jersey, and Uga III wore it to the next Georgia home game—where, unfortunately, it rained. That was a problem because Swann and Deborah had employed a student's mentality, buying the cheapest red shirt they could find—which bled in the downpour.

"When the game ended and Uga III's shirt was removed," Cecelia recalls, "we were left with a sorry-looking bulldog. Swann had to keep him inside until she could get the dye out of his coat. For a week, Georgia had a pink mascot!"

Uga III is oblivious to this pre-game plea from Tennessee's mascot, Smokey—a blue tick coon hound, if y'all can believe there is such a thing—who said he hoped the Bulldogs would take it easy on the Vols. They didn't. Georgia won both games in Knoxville during Uga III's tenure, including the 1980 season opener that marked the historic debut of Herschel Walker.

Standing up to the LSU tiger

Foreign fields of battle held no fear for Georgia football teams during Uga III's watch. They traveled to Neyland Stadium twice and beat the Tennessee Vols both times. They had winning records at South Carolina's Cockpit and at Georgia Tech's Grant Field—winning in Atlanta in the rain, in the cold, and on Thanksgiving night before a national TV audience. They really cleaned up in Jacksonville, beating Florida seven times during Uga III's nine seasons on the job. And in winning the SEC championship in 1976, Georgia took care of all of its rivals, beating Clemson, South Carolina, Florida, Auburn, and Georgia Tech in the same year—and, for good measure, Alabama, too.

In 1978, during Uga III's only trip to Baton Rouge, Georgia ran into an unbeaten, sixth-ranked team led by All-America running back Charles Alexander. The Tigers are always tough to beat on Saturday nights in the Bayou, and Alexander made them doubly dangerous. But thanks to Uga III, Vince Dooley had an inkling prior to the game that this would be the Bulldogs' night. In fact, the moment made such an impression on Dooley that he recalled it on his Athens radio show twenty years later, as Georgia was preparing for a game in Baton Rouge against another sixth-ranked LSU team. Dooley's '98 radio commentary went like this:

"Later that year [1978], we went down to play the Bengal Tigers in Baton Rouge. Just prior to the game, I was out on the field while the team was dressing and I noticed that out of the end zone came LSU's mascot, Mike the tiger, in a cage. The LSU fans went berserk, especially when the cheerleaders poked him in the ribs. They stuck a microphone up to the cage and he let out a big roar.

"They rolled the cage toward the 50-yard line, where the tiger normally stays during a game—and right in his path was Uga III,

Leaving the Gator Bowl after one of Georgia's seven victories against Florida over a nine-year span, Vince Dooley gets a police escort from state trooper Bobby Clifton with Sonny and Uga III in hot pursuit.

Uga III giving Sonny some "sugar."

which really infuriated the tiger. He ran up to the front of his cage and let out a loud roar—but ol' Uga just sat there. That really made the tiger mad. He got up on his hind legs, rattled the cage, and roared even louder. When the tiger did that, Uga raised up, took two steps forward, and barked—at which time the tiger sheepishly retreated to the back of the cage."

Dooley concluded his radio show by saying:

"I got so excited that I ran into the dressing room and told the team, 'Let's go, men . . . we've got 'em tonight!'"

The Dogs took Dooley at his word, upsetting LSU 24-17 back in '78 and going on to a 9-2-1 finish and a No. 16 ranking in the polls.

And twenty years later, with Uga III's grandson, Uga V, patrolling the sidelines and keeping Mike the tiger in his place, Georgia again beat LSU in Baton Rouge, this time by a 28-27 score.

The reason you don't give a bulldog turkey skin

Two weeks after the LSU game in '78, Georgia edged Kentucky 17-16 on a cold night in Lexington. To ward off the post-game chill, Sonny hooked up with friend and amateur chef Jack "The visiting coach from Shanghai Tech" Peng, who had roasted a turkey and stashed it in the trunk of his car.

"Jack had some cold beers in a cooler," says Sonny, "and the

three of us—me, Jack, and Coach Bill Hartman—had a nice little post-game party there in the parking lot waiting for the team to shower and dress."

Actually, there were four Georgia faithful at that Lexington tailgater, and Uga III managed to coax more than his share of turkey skin out of Jack Peng and Coach Hartman. Sonny and Uga then flew with the team to Atlanta, where they spent the night at the AirHost Inn before boarding a plane for Savannah Sunday morning.

"I checked us into the room, set the alarm for 5 A.M., and fell asleep as soon as I hit the pillow," says Sonny, who was so exhausted he didn't bother hooking Uga to the leg of the bed. Bad move. "In the middle of the night, I woke up to this highly unpleasant odor. I became aware that Uga was sleeping at the foot of my bed, and when I turned on the light I discovered that he had done the unthinkable right there in my bed! It looked like something out of a horror movie! I threw the bedspread in the bathtub and did my best to get out the worst of it. I could've killed that dog, but then I remembered . . . the turkey skin from Lexington had exacted its revenge!"

Uga III embodied the Bulldog rallying cry, "Hunker down!"
No wonder Mike the LSU tiger was intimidated.

Uga III

'. . .Try To Run Over Me Willya!'

When freshman quarterback Buck Belue rallied Georgia from a 20-0 deficit to beat Georgia Tech 29-28 in 1978, Atlanta newspaper cartoonist Baldy penned this drawing of Uga III wrecking the Ramblin' Wreck.

In 1979, Uga III was selected by the Albany China Company, Ltd. of Worcester, England, to be immortalized in its famous series of animal figurines. He was the only college mascot on a short list that included Triple Crown winners Secretariat, Seattle Slew, and Affirmed. To create a faithful rendering, artist Neil Campbell flew to Savannah from England to study Uga III.

Undefeated, untied, undisputed, undenied

The National Championship season surprised just about everyone, as even the most optimistic fan would have been hard-pressed to envision what happened to the Georgia football team in 1980.

"Thinking back on it now, it's just amazing that it happened the way it did," says Sonny, who was celebrating his twenty-fifth season with the mascots. "After all, our '79 team had been destroyed by Virginia 31-0 at Homecoming, and only a 16-3 victory over Tech prevented Coach Dooley from suffering what would have been only the second losing season of his coaching career. From that humble beginning—and with a lot of help from Herschel—we managed to win it all."

Historic accomplishments were not in the scouting report for the 1980 team, which had to open the season at night in Knoxville against heavily favored Tennessee and 96,000 screaming Vols fans. Trailing 15-0 in the third quarter, Vince Dooley put the game in a freshman's hands. Herschel Walker, from Wrightsville, Georgia, had been one of the most sought-after high school recruits in the nation. But his eighty-six touchdowns and 6,137 prep rushing yards had come against small-town Class A opposition.

How well Walker would do against major college defenses was a mystery. Those questions were quickly answered when No. 34 took a handoff in the third quarter of the Tennessee game and literally ran over Vols defensive back—and future Dallas Cowboy teammate—Bill Bates en route to a 15-yard touchdown. Walker later scored on a 9-yard run and Rex Robinson kicked the crucial extra point as Georgia shocked Tennessee 16-15.

"We were all there for those theatrics—me, Cecelia, Charles, and Uga III," says Sonny. "It was his final year as mascot, but it was one for the history books."

Nine weeks later, all eyes were on Georgia—still undefeated and ranked No. 2 in the polls—as the Dogs traveled to Jacksonville for their annual shootout with the Florida Gators. Georgia was heavily favored, but with time running out in the fourth quarter Florida led 21-20.

"I knew I had to get Uga III out of the stadium before the end of the game," says Sonny, "so I walked behind the Florida bench and across the southern end zone. The Dogs were backed up to their own goal line at the opposite end of the field, and our chances of pulling out the game—and keeping our National Championship

Uga III

hopes alive—seemed remote. Uga was at the opposite end of the field with Charles, and I remember him saying later that Uga seemed in no hurry to leave the stadium. Which was funny because it was a warm day and he's usually anxious to go by the fourth quarter. But not that day in Florida. Did Uga III sense something big was about to happen?"

With little more than a minute left on the clock, quarterback Buck Belue took the snap from his own 7-yard line, avoided tacklers who nearly trapped him in the end zone for a safety, and drifted out in the right flat looking for a miracle. He found one in Lindsay Scott, the wide receiver-track star who made a jumping catch of Belue's pass and set sail for the distant end zone.

"As Lindsay streaked down the left sideline, I was suddenly in the thick of the action because he was coming right at me!" says Sonny. "When he crossed the goal line, he was mobbed by players and Georgia fans—and, if you look closely at photos of that scene, you'll find me in the midst of the sideline pandemonium. It was the greatest play in Georgia history, and there was so much noise and commotion that it was all I could do to find Uga and Charles."

Uga III

Georgia's dramatic 26-21 victory over Florida, coupled with a hard-earned 31-21 win at Auburn the following week, clinched the SEC championship. Two weeks later in Athens, the Dogs beat Georgia Tech 38-20 to finish the regular season 11-0, setting the stage for a National Championship game against Notre Dame in the Sugar Bowl in New Orleans.

"Requests for pictures of Uga III began pouring in from all over the country," says Sonny. "He was like a national hero!"

The cover of The Georgia Bulldog:

Go You Silver Britches!
UGA's Silver Anniversary
Texas A&M Scouting Report
Clemson Scouting Report

The Georgia BULLDOG

Volume 31 — Number 1 $1.50

Happy Anniversary UGA!

The 1980 season, which was destined to bring so much glory to the Georgia football program, marked the mascots' twenty-fifth season dating back to Uga I's debut in 1956—and Uga III's last hurrah.

Kent Hannon's story in the November 3, 1980, issue of *Sports Illustrated* awakened the rest of the country to what the SEC already knew—that Herschel Walker was the most amazing freshman in college football history.

by Kent Hannon

COLLEGE FOOTBALL

The latest peach from Georgia

Frosh Running Back Herschel Walker makes Bulldog rivals look like the pits

Criminology major Walker and classmate Megan Holland work in the library on a gun control report.

This photo of Uga III was taken on a momentous day in Georgia football history—November 1, 1980—when Herschel Walker outdueled eventual Heisman Trophy winner George Rogers of South Carolina on national TV. Georgia won the game 13-10 to set up its date with destiny in Jacksonville the following week.

When Lindsay Scott set sail for the end zone against Florida on the most famous play in Georgia football history, his path took him directly toward Sonny, who was screaming just as loud as Larry Munson from his vantage point in the end zone (see red arrow). The victory vaulted Georgia to No. 1 in the polls, and Herschel moved up to the cover of *Sports Illustrated*.

Sonny and Uga's year-end card left no doubt as to what they wanted for Christmas—and New Year's.

Uga III

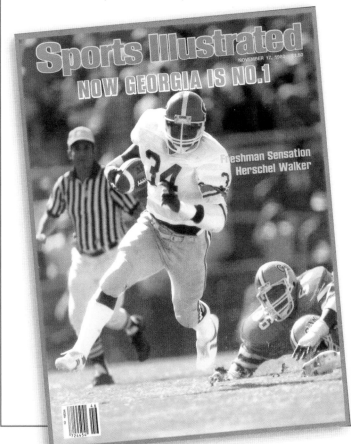

Georgia's 1981 Sugar Bowl media guide.

Against Notre Dame in the National Championship game, Herschel Walker gained 150 yards and scored two touchdowns—this one providing the margin of victory in a 17-10 victory and a perfect 12-0 record.

Toast of Bourbon Street

Accompanied by their close friends, Barron Burke and his wife Laura, the Seilers—Sonny, Cecelia, Charles, and Uga III—flew to New Orleans with UGA president Fred Davison and his party and checked into the Fairmont Hotel on Canal Street, which was also team headquarters. Uga III was invited to and attended most of the social affairs put on by the Sugar Bowl, and at night he attracted a large following as the Seilers walked him through the French Quarter in his traditional red jersey and spiked collar.

Georgia had been playing football since 1892, and Notre Dame since 1887—but the two schools had never met on the gridiron until the night of January 1, 1981, in a jam-packed Superdome.

"There was a lot of room for Uga on the sidelines," says Sonny, "and we had a great view of that bungled kickoff return

when Notre Dame allowed a Savannah kid out of Benedictine, Bob Kelly, to recover a free ball on the Notre Dame 2-yard line to set up the Dogs' first touchdown."

Herschel Walker's 150 rushing yards were a huge factor because the Irish defense held the rest of the team to 30 yards on the ground and just 7 through the air. Herschel scored two touchdowns, Rex Robinson kicked a field goal, and Georgia won the biggest game it had ever played by a score of 17-10 to win the National Championship.

"As the game ended, Uga and I had to run for our lives to escape the sea of Georgia fans who poured onto the field to celebrate," Sonny recalls. "We barely made it to the Georgia dressing room, where we shared in a celebration that seemed to go on forever. I wish I had a dollar for every person who gave Uga III a pat on the head that night."

Sense of smell saves Uga III's eyesight

The National Championship game was Uga III's crowning moment as the Georgia mascot. His final appearance would come in Athens the following September, and it would be his last, owing in part to a chronic eye problem.

"Shortly before the 1979 season, we began to notice a discharge in Uga III's right eye," says Sonny. "For awhile, we would simply wipe it out and wash it with a solution of warm, clear water. When it became apparent we were losing the battle, we took him to the UGA vet school, where he was diagnosed with a condition commonly known as dry eye."

UGA veterinarians explained that Uga's condition was caused by the failure of his tear ducts to keep his eye moist. It was unusual for English bulldogs to suffer from dry eye, they said, and, left untreated, it could cause blindness.

"For awhile, we tried to control it by applying artificial tears," says Sonny, "and then by using an ointment that would lubricate the eyelids and keep Uga III's eye moist when he blinked. But it required three or four treatments a day, and by morning his eye would be completely closed."

Doctors at the UGA vet school solved the problem with a new

In 1979, doctors at the UGA vet school alleviated a dry eye condition in Uga III's right eye by creating an artificial tear duct from a saliva gland. In this photo, taken a year later, muscles on the top of Uga III's head had begun to atrophy, causing his left eye to recede somewhat but not affecting his vision.

and innovative technique. With Uga III under general anesthesia, veterinary surgeons created an artificial tear duct by taking a minute portion of a saliva gland from his throat and transplanting it beneath his eyelid—where it would produce tears whenever he smelled or sensed food.

"As bizarre as it sounds, it worked!" says Sonny. "Within forty-eight hours, the surgery was producing 'tears' whenever Uga III sensed food—at times, too many tears. If you dangled a piece of food near his face, his right eye would run like a faucet. It would actually make a small puddle on the floor! All bulldogs like sweets, but we don't give these dogs many treats because it's not good for them. But whenever Uga heard the crinkle of cellophane wrappers, he identified it with candy—even if it was just Cecelia putting crackers on the table for soup—and we'd have to mop up the puddle before we could eat."

The new tear duct saved Uga III's eyesight, but took its toll cosmetically. Thinking of bulldogs as handsome is an acquired taste, but there is a definite symmetry to their crinkled, heavily jowled faces. In Uga III's case, the makeshift tear duct caused his right cheek to be constantly moist and matted.

Uga III

"It left a brown stain under his eye that made him look a little less attractive, I guess you could say—but maybe a little more rough and tumble, too," says Sonny. "Fortunately, he never lost his eyesight—and for that, we have his sense of smell and his appetite to thank!"

In 1980, muscles on the top of Uga III's head began to atrophy. Doctors could find no medical explanation and no cure. But again, the problem was purely cosmetic. The condition caused Uga III's left eye to recede somewhat, but it didn't affect his eyesight, which enabled him to make it through the historic 1980 season.

When it comes to staying in good health, the mascots' first line of defense has always been their Savannah veterinarian, Ben Page. When Uga III (shown here with Dr. Page and Charles Seiler) developed an eye problem in 1979, Dr. Page, a Georgia grad, recommended that the Seilers take him to the UGA vet school.

Feted at the Capitol

R ecognition comes easy—and from all directions—when you're No. 1. One of Uga III's most unique and rewarding experiences came in January 1981, when he accompanied the 1980 National Championship team and Georgia coaches to the state capitol in Atlanta to be recognized by the Georgia General Assembly.

Representative and Georgia alumnus Bob Argo of Athens made arrangements through Speaker of the House Tom Murphy for the players, coaches, and mascot to march into the legislative chambers.

"When the clerk announced the team," says Cecelia, "Uga, Sonny, and I led the procession into the state house chambers to a standing ovation by the state representatives. A resolution was read commending the members of the Georgia football team on the National Championship."

"Speaker Murphy is a University of Georgia graduate who has shown great affection for all of the Georgia mascots," says Sonny. "The speaker has traveled with us to numerous bowl games, and he's never too busy to come over and give the dogs a friendly pat."

After Uga III's appearance at the Capitol, Speaker Murphy showed his droll sense of humor by telling the press, "This is the first time that a dog has been allowed in the house chambers . . . a four-legged dog, that is."

(above) With a packed gallery lending their applause, Uga III and Cecelia led the National Champions through the Georgia General Assembly, where they were honored by state lawmakers for their 12-0 season in 1980. (top left) Afterward, the Seilers and the dog of the hour posed with state rep. Bob Argo (left) and Georgia play-by-play man Larry Munson (right).

Uga III

Uga III

Retirement gala an RSVP occasion

On January 8, 1981, after much discussion, Sonny and Cecelia decided it was in the best interest of the university and Uga III for him to retire in the fall. They wrote a letter to Coach Dooley, citing Uga's many accomplishments and his health problems, which now included arthritis.

"We knew that by September he wouldn't be able to perform," says Sonny. "Coach Dooley agreed with our decision. But at the time, it still wasn't known who would replace Uga III—who had never sired an all-white pup."

To mark Uga III's impending retirement, the Seilers went first class. They booked the Savannah Golf Club for the night of February 6, 1981, and sent out printed invitations. The guest list included diehard Georgia football fans and friends who really cared about Uga. The Seilers sent out 400 invitations, and almost everyone came. Those who couldn't sent nice notes expressing regrets and appreciation for Uga III.

"Should anyone ask, 'Has the Savannah Golf Club gone to the dogs,'" said general manager Chuck Witherspoon, "say, 'Yes, but with reservations!'"

In deference to the guest of honor, the caterers created a special centerpiece on the hors d'oeuvres table. It consisted of prime rib bones held in place by dog food and garnished with dog biscuits and hamburger patties. A sign next to the centerpiece noted that it was reserved for "genuine hunker-down bull-dawgs only." Two-legged guests had to settle for meat balls and chicken wings.

Midway through the party, the guest of honor arrived, wearing his red jersey and spiked collar. The Seilers' youngest daughter Sara kept Uga III company while partygoers came by to pat the nine-year-old bulldog on the head and have their photo taken with him.

The highlight of the evening was Savannah mayor John Rousakis, another UGA alumnus, presenting Uga III with the key to the city. Sonny accepted it on behalf of Uga, and the entire assemblage stood and applauded.

"Uga III pricked up his ears as if he knew it was all for him," says Sonny. "It was an evening we will never forget."

The Seilers cordially invite you
to a reception for

UGA III

in honor of his retirement
next Fall as official Mascot
of the University of Georgia. . .
the undefeated, untied,
undisputed and undenied

National Champion
of College Football
for 1980

Feburary 6, 1981
7:00 p.m. to 8:30 p.m.
Savannah Golf Club
President Street Extension
Savannah, Georgia

RSVP to the Seilers
421 East 44th Street
Savannah, Georgia 31405
or to Ms. Henderson
(912) 236-2491

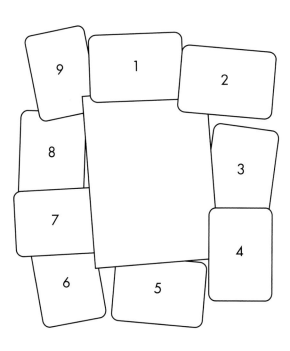

1. Savannah's late mayor John Rousakis presents Sonny (and Uga III, at left) with a key to the city.

2. The three men are (from left) Tom Coffey, retired sports editor of the *Savannah Morning News;* Joe Saseen, a former law associate of Sonny's; and "patron saint of the Seiler children," and retired businessman Dickie Eskedor.

3. Savannah businessman Homer Peeples and wife Ruth.

4. The couple in the middle are Esther and Ed Shaver, who own Shaver's bookstore on Madison Square in Savannah. On either side of them are Savannah's late city manager Don Mendonza and wife Susan.

5. (from left) Retired investor Billy McKenna, his daughter Virginia, and James W. Head, retired judge of the Chatham County Superior Court.

6. Beth Daniel, who works for the juvenile court system in Savannah, was among those who later accompanied the Seilers—and Uga IV—to Herschel Walker's Heisman Trophy banquet in New York.

7. (from left) Laura Burke, who owns Pickles Deli in Savannah, and Cecelia and Charles Seiler.

8. The Seilers' youngest daughter, Sara Story, holds the key to the city. That's author Reds Helmey in the background.

9. Dr. Julian Quattlebaum Sr., a former president of the UGA alumni society, helped save Uga I's life by getting him an appointment with heartworm specialists at the Medical College of Georgia.

When it came time for Uga III to retire, the Seilers held a gala reception in his honor at the Savannah Golf Club. See above for names of the guests in these photos.

Quest for an all-white pup

By the spring of 1981, Uga III's arthritis prevented him from running and restricted his walking. He was now on daily medication, but otherwise in good spirits.

In late June, Uga III began to experience equilibrium problems. UGA veterinarians detected a growth in his throat. By late July, it was diagnosed as cancer. He was too old for chemotherapy, and as the days went by he became very passive. He showed some signs of senility, but continued to recognize his family and respond to his name.

"We had planned to have Uga III retired at the 1981 season opener," says Sonny, "but we began to wonder whether he would make it that long. The weaker he became, the more it looked like Otto might have to step in."

Although he fathered numerous litters, Uga III had never sired an all-white male pup. In December 1978, a near-perfect dog named Otto was born [see p. 84]. He was mostly white, except for a brown-and-black spot on his back that ran down his hindquarters to his tail.

"Otto was a great dog, and I thought he was going to have to serve," says Sonny, "but we decided to mate Uga III one last time with a female bulldog in Flagler Beach, Florida, who had never had puppies."

Bulldog litters sometimes consist of as many as a half-dozen puppies. The union between aging Uga III and the female from Flagler Beach produced just one offspring, who was born in March 1981—but, as luck would have it, that puppy was an all-white male who was promptly dubbed Uga IV.

"Much like the teams he served," says Sonny, "Uga III 'pulled it out' in the twilight of his career."

Newspaper headlines around the South heralded the new mascot's arrival, and just six months later, though still on puppy chow, Uga IV had to assume center stage (see p. 71-72).

Uga III

Uga III

So long, Uga III!

The pre-game retirement ceremony at the '81 season opener against Tennessee had to be carefully planned because, by that time, Uga III couldn't walk; it was all he could do to stand for a few minutes at a time. While the Sanford Stadium announcer listed Uga III's accomplishments, Sonny drove him onto the field in a golf cart. Uga III rested comfortably in Charles's lap, while Cecelia, Bess, and Sara walked behind.

Uga IV, on the other hand, was eager to get started. He seemed unaware of his aging father, who, just nine months before, was part of a National Championship. As the two dogs met at midfield and the P.A. announcer concluded his remarks, 82,000 people broke into the familiar chant that was born fifteen years earlier at Uga I's retirement—only in plural this time, shouting:

"Damn Good Dogs! Damn Good Dogs! Damn Good Dogs!"

For one brief moment, Uga III raised his head, as if to acknowledge the cheers, then settled back in Charles' lap.

Uga III was too old and too sick to walk onto the field for his retirement ceremony at the season opener in 1981, so Sonny drove him onto the field in a golf cart. Uga III rested comfortably in Charles' lap while Cecelia, Sara, and Bess walked behind.

Champion of the Canine Race

To all our gallant Ugas—Hail!
Long may their mascot line prevail,
So always on the field there'll be,
Another like ONE—TWO or THREE.

We are gathered here for this great game,
To retire THREE with all his fame.
Since starting as a young beginner,
He's proved himself to be a winner.

Twice he's won the S.E.C.,
And then his team moved on to be
The National Champions—undenied,
Swelling us with ardent pride.

The pinnacle of this mascot's fame
Was the victory over Notre Dame,
For then his team was true and tried,
Undefeated and untied.

We're ever grateful to Uga THREE,
No grander mascot could there be.
With other stars he takes his place,
As champion of the canine race.

Though old and halt and almost blind,
He showed the grit of bulldog-kind,
At every game where he appeared;
And knowing how he persevered,
The fans have greeted him with cheers,
As reigning mascot for ten years.

As victory after victory came,
Bestowing honor on his name,
The sun shone brightly o'er his head,
Good fortune on his team was shed.

Now the sun is sinking low.
It's time for UGA THREE to go,
Drifting toward a peaceful shore,
To leave a place for UGA FOUR.

—David C. Barrow Jr.

Uga III

Uga III elected to *Animals Who's Who*

*A*nimals Who's Who is a book written by Ruthven Tremain, who taught physics at Wesleyan University and worked as a researcher at *Time* magazine. Her book features celebrated animals in history, popular culture, literature, and lore. In early 1983, two and a half years after Uga III's death, the Seilers were notified that he would be listed in this directory of famous animals—along with Mickey Mouse, the Cowardly Lion, and Morris the Cat. Also listed

Uga III

were Snoopy, Checkers, the Trojan Horse, Dumbo, Man O'War, Moby Dick, Heathcliff, Benji, and the White Rabbit from *Alice's Adventures in Wonderland*.

On September 22, 1981, Uga III died peacefully in his bed at the Seilers' home in Ardsley Park, Savannah.

The following day, Sonny and Charles took him on his last trip to Athens. The graves of Uga I and Uga II had been relocated from the east end of Sanford Stadium to make way for construction that would enclose that end. The graves were now located in the dirt embankment near Dr. Sanford's bust at the west end of the south stands.

"It was a cool autumn day, the kind Uga III relished," says Sonny. "He was lowered into the ground in a red wooden coffin. It's always hard to say goodbye to a good friend, but this dog was special. We had been to the mountaintop together, and none of us would ever forget him."

Affixed to the top of the coffin, engraved in brass, was a simple "1." Nothing else was needed.

Sonny being interviewed by the press at the funeral of Uga III, whose coffin was adorned with the appropriate number for a National Championship dog: 1.

UGA III

GEORGIA MASCOT
1972-1981
TWO S.E.C. CHAMPIONSHIPS
SIX BOWL TEAMS
THE UNDEFEATED, UNTIED,
UNDISPUTED AND
UNDENIED
NATIONAL CHAMPION
OF COLLEGE FOOTBALL 1980
"HOW 'BOUT THIS DOG"

Uga IV
1981–90

Born
March 18, 1981

AKC registered name
Seiler's Uga Four

Dates of service
September 5, 1981
to December 30, 1989

Football record
73-25-4

SEC titles
2
1981 (10-2)
1982 (11-1)

Bowl record
3-4-2
lost to Pittsburgh 24-20
in '82 Sugar Bowl

lost to Penn State 27-23
in '83 Sugar Bowl

beat Texas 10-9 in
'84 Cotton Bowl

tied Florida State 17-17
in '84 Citrus Bowl

tied Arizona 13-13 in
'85 Sun Bowl

lost to Boston College 27-24
in '86 Hall of Fame Bowl

beat Arkansas 20-17
in '87 Liberty Bowl

beat Michigan State 34-27
in '88 Gator Bowl

lost to Syracuse 19-18
in '89 Peach Bowl

Died
February 27, 1990

Epitaph
"The Dog of the Decade"

Uga IV

Georgia's Winningest Lead Dog

When Uga IV replaced his famous father at the 1981 season opener against Tennessee in Athens, he was just six months old—the youngest of the six mascots to serve. Seamstress Nonie Sutton had to cut down one of Uga III's shirts to fit him, and it would be another year before the fourth mascot in the line was big enough to wear the famous spiked collar.

But Uga IV was a huge hit with Georgia fans from the moment he trotted onto the field on September 5, 1981. So spirited was his performance that day—as Georgia was demolishing Tennessee 44-0—that it brought to mind Vince Dooley's comments about another famous freshman, Herschel Walker, who had made his debut a year earlier against Tennessee:

Uga IV was a natural with people, full of energy, and always ready to travel—which was fortunate since Georgia went to a bowl game all nine years that he served as mascot. And when Herschel Walker won the Heisman in 1982, Uga IV made history, too.

"We put him in and he didn't know where he was supposed to go. Or when to make his move. He was just taking off *running*— as if for the sheer joy of it!"

"It's the same with a new dog," says Sonny. "As heartsick as you are to lose a long-time friend and member of the family, it's the exuberance of the next pup in line that gets you through it, keeps you looking to the future."

Georgia's future was brighter than ever. The Dogs finished the 1981 season 10-1, won another SEC championship, and earned a second consecutive trip to the Sugar Bowl. The '82 team went them one better, winning all eleven regular-season games, adding a third conference title in a row and a third straight Sugar Bowl berth.

"Looking back at those two teams," says Sonny, "the Dogs were a play away from winning a second National Championship in '81 when Pitt's Dan Marino beat us with that touchdown pass in the final minute of the Sugar Bowl. And we just missed another one in '82, losing a close game to Penn State after entering the Sugar Bowl 11-0. We could have won three National Championships in a row— something no college football team has ever achieved—and Uga IV was a part of all that excitement. He was a natural with people, full of energy, and always ready to travel—which was fortunate because Georgia went to a bowl game in every one of Uga IV's nine years as mascot."

The news media took an immediate liking to Uga IV, and Georgia's numerous appearances on TV—forty-three national and nine regional telecasts from 1981– 89—were highlighted by shots of Uga IV patrolling the sidelines or cooling off in his fireplug.

Bands and crowd noise never fazed this dog. He seemed to sense his responsibility and, as he grew in stature, he also grew in popularity.

Which is not to say he never made a mistake.

Uga IV

Like a mighty oak that grows from a tiny acorn, bulldogs start out like toy versions of themselves (see p. 71). Far from full-grown when he succeeded his dad at the '81 season-opener (see photos with Cecelia and sisters Bess and Sara Seiler), Uga IV had finally grown into the spiked collar when he posed with cheerleader Marty Argo.

[THEY SAID IT]

"AS CELEBRITIES GO, he isn't much to look at. He's short, squatty and bowlegged. He has a corrugated face and a pug nose and wide, dropping chops. Give him a cigar and he would look like Edward G. Robinson. His name could be Spike, or Butch, or Little Caesar. But Georgia football fans know the lovable school mascot as Uga IV.

—David Casstevens, *Dallas Morning News*

Uga christens new Vandy carpet

"During the 1981 season, Vanderbilt had just installed new artificial turf in its football stadium," Sonny recalls. "Artificial turf was the hot new thing back then—and very expensive. Uga IV was a freshman at the time, and on his first trip to Nashville he acted like one."

At away games, it was Coach Dooley's policy to bus the team directly to the stadium for a walk-through on the field. Sometimes the team would change into sweats and work out for about forty minutes to get the kinks out of their legs. That was the case on the Friday before the '81 Vandy game, as Dooley wanted his team to get a feel for the new Astroturf field.

Vanderbilt's athletic director, Roy Kramer, who went on to become commissioner of the Southeastern Conference, took Dooley on a tour of the new carpet. Both men smiled when Dee Matthews of the Albany (Georgia) Bulldog Club came walking by with Uga IV on the leash—when suddenly, to Kramer's horror, Uga committed a flagrant breach of social etiquette on Vandy's high-priced—and previously spotless—emerald turf!

For perhaps thirty seconds, Kramer and Dooley stood there in awkward, embarrassed silence, neither man knowing what to say.

Finally, Dooley, who likes to refer to the mascots as though they're players, decided to play it for laughs, saying:

"That dawg . . . has no discipline."

Kramer got over it. But according to Georgia's sports information director Claude Felton, his counterpart at Vandy has always suspected that someone slipped Uga some doggie Ex-Lax to promote his misbehavior.

"I'd like to say that was the only time Uga misbehaved at Vandy," says Sonny, "but I can't forget the time Bob Bishop, a prominent Athens banker and longtime member of the UGA Athletic Board, offered to take Uga's leash while we were unpacking the team bus at the Vanderbilt stadium."

What Bishop didn't realize is that, upon occasion, Uga will display what Sonny calls "excessive affection" for a friend or fan—particularly if they're female.

"On this occasion," says Sonny, "an adoring woman stooped down to pet Uga, who promptly wrapped his front legs around one of hers. Poor Bob wasn't sure what to do, and a team manager had to come to her rescue. It was the last time Bob ever volunteered to tend Uga's leash."

Uga IV

Co-stars: Herschel and Uga

The Heisman Trophy is the most coveted prize in college football, and Herschel Walker could have—probably should have—won it as a freshman at Georgia.

In 1980, a year removed from Class A high school football, Herschel led the Dogs to a 12-0 record and the National Championship. And he did it with offensive fireworks almost every Saturday. He bested eventual Heisman winner George Rogers in a stunning head-to-head battle with South Carolina's senior running back on national TV (219 yards to 168). But no freshman has ever won the Heisman, and that sentiment helped Rogers prevail in the balloting with Herschel finishing third, behind Rogers and Pittsburgh linebacker Hugh Green.

With defenses crowding the line of scrimmage to try to contain him as a sophomore, Herschel managed to increase his rushing yardage from 1,616 to 1,891. Included in that total were three remarkable statistics that showed how much better he performed as a sophomore: 108 first-down runs (vs. 58 in '80), 72 runs of at least 10 yards (vs. 35 in '80), and twenty touchdowns (vs. fifteen in '80). Unfortunately, Southern Cal's Marcus Allen set an NCAA record with 2,342 rushing yards in '81, relegating Herschel to second place in the Heisman balloting.

Fortunately, sustained excellence has a way of winning out, and on December 4, 1982, the Downtown Athletic Club in New York announced what the college football world had known all along—that Herschel Walker was the finest player in the country. As a junior, he gained 1,752 yards, scored seventeen touchdowns—and he did so while wearing a cast to protect his broken thumb for the first three games. Herschel's three-year rushing total of 5,097 yards was an NCAA record. And in winning the '82 Heisman, he bested two future NFL greats, Stanford's John Elway and SMU's Eric Dickerson, in the voting.

The Heisman banquet—a black-tie affair that attracts past winners plus 1,200 invited guests—was scheduled for December 9 at the New York Hilton. Traditionally, the recipient gets to invite two teammates. Herschel selected defensive back Darryl Jones and fullback Chris McCarthy, who had blocked for Herschel during his Heisman-winning season.

There was one other guest who got a special invitation: Uga IV!

Uga IV

Herschel Walker with his father, Sonny, and Uga IV at Picture Day in August 1981.

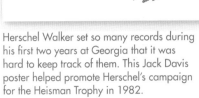

Herschel Walker set so many records during his first two years at Georgia that it was hard to keep track of them. This Jack Davis poster helped promote Herschel's campaign for the Heisman Trophy in 1982.

Uga IV

No player in college football history has loomed larger than No. 34, who was named Offensive Player of the Century by CBS Sports. If he hadn't turned pro a year early, Herschel would have obliterated the NCAA career rushing record and likely surpassed 7,000 yards.

Heisman trip to New York

Sonny, his law partner, Brice Ladson, and Uga IV flew to New York on Delta Airlines. Also aboard that flight were Herschel Walker and members of his immediate family, including his mother and father, his three brothers and three sisters. Herschel's high school coach from Wrightsville, Gary Phillips, was also aboard.

"When we arrived in New York, we all rode from the airport to the hotel in a shuttle bus arranged by the Downtown Athletic Club," Sonny recalls. "When we got to the New York Hilton, at Fifty-fourth and Avenue of the Americas, just south of Central Park, I instinctively looked around for a patch of grass for Uga to visit. He had been cooped up on the plane for several hours, and I knew he was due for the pause that refreshes. Central Park was five blocks away, but fortunately he found a suitable place around the corner of the building, albeit solid concrete."

Sonny wasn't sure what role Uga IV would play in the Heisman festivities. But Nonie Sutton had made a white collar, which fit neatly around his neck. Attached to the collar was his obligatory black tie. He had his picture taken by several photographers in the lobby of the Hilton the morning before the banquet, but Uga IV and Sonny spent most of the day relaxing in their room at the Hilton. The temperature outside was in the twenties, which is extremely cold for a short-haired pooch who hails from South Georgia. But by 4 P.M., Uga needed to go out.

"We walked up to Central Park," says Sonny, "and by the time we got there, we were both exhausted. Those New York blocks are tough on a dog with short legs and an owner twenty-five years removed from his collegiate swimming days."

And the effort was all for naught, as Uga IV was more interested in chasing Central Park pigeons than in taking care of business.

Returning to the Hilton, Sonny started getting ready for the banquet, while Uga IV fell asleep on the floor. The phone rang. It was Georgia's sports information director Claude Felton, who was in charge of the arrangements for the Georgia contingent. He had prearranged Uga's visit to the anteroom off of the main ballroom, where all of the past Heisman Trophy winners congregate for fellowship and cocktails prior to the banquet.

Herschel finally got his Heisman in '82, and Sonny and Uga IV were there at the Downtown Athletic Club in New York City to share the moment with him—Uga being the only mascot ever to be so honored. Back home (see p.77), the good people of Wrightsville showed how proud they were of their native son.

Sonny was instructed to bring Uga to the mezzanine floor, where they would be met by security at the elevator and ushered to the anteroom for photographs. Uga looked resplendent in his traditional red jersey topped off by his white collar and black tie. When he and Sonny arrived at the photo room, they were greeted by Felton, who gave Sonny a Heisman badge and nameplate.

"One glance around the room was like a trip back in football history," Sonny recalls. "I'm talking Doc Blanchard and Glenn Davis of Army, Johnny Lujack and Leon Hart of Notre Dame, Doak Walker of SMU—players I had worshipped as a kid."

But the man of the hour was Herschel Walker, who was surrounded by sports writers from all over the nation and by still photographers, whose flash bulbs lit up the room.

"Uga IV was working the room pretty good himself," says Sonny, "when the president of the Downtown Athletic Club took him by the leash and walked him right into the massive ballroom, which was all set up for the banquet."

Sonny was both heartened and somewhat astonished that Uga IV was being treated like the rest of the honored guests—when suddenly he had a distressing thought:

Uga did nothing in Central Park . . . what if he misbehaves right here at the Heisman banquet!

Fortunately, Uga IV conducted himself like a perfect gentleman, leaving the Hilton carpet just the way he had found it.

When the president of the Downtown Athletic Club led Uga IV back into the anteroom, the Heisman winners of the past were lining up in order of the year they had won the trophy.

The grand entrance parade is a spectacle in itself. Large banners from every Heisman winner's school encircle the hall. While these legends of the past were lining up, one of them broke ranks and came over to give Uga IV a friendly pat. It was then-Florida coach Steve Spurrier.

"Despite his infamous reputation among Bulldog faithful," says Sonny, "I still have a soft spot in my heart for Steve because of his kind and friendly recognition of our mascot."

In the banquet hall, a band began playing "I Wanna Be a Football Hero" and the grand parade started moving. Each past winner was announced as he came through the doorway to take his place at the head table, which had been structured in three tiers with a podium in the middle.

When the parade ended, Sonny took Uga IV up to their hotel room and relieved him of his white collar, black tie, and red shirt. Fortunately, Uga was exhausted and slept peacefully until Sonny returned later in the evening.

The Heisman dinner was a splendid affair. Multiple courses were served while introductions were made from the head table. The dessert was baked Alaska, which was served at tableside as Herschel was being presented with the trophy. Coach Dooley responded eloquently on behalf of the University of Georgia, and then the ultra-modest award-winner expressed his appreciation, while giving a great deal of the credit to his team.

"The Heisman banquet was especially meaningful to me," says Sonny, "because a group of Georgia fans from Savannah—who were in New York with the Homebuilders Association—managed to get tickets to the banquet and share the experience with us."

When the banquet ended, Sonny and the Savannah contingent—which included Dick and Judy Coleman, Tom and Mary Ellen Beytagh, Jimmy and Barbie Wilson, and Beth and Sidney Daniel—were in the mood to party.

"We took Uga IV with us for a night on the town," says Sonny, "and we ended up at Studio 54, which was all the rage back then.

Uga IV

A bouncer the size of Herschel stopped us at the door, and not even Uga's presence was enough to get us past him."

The next day, an AP photo of Herschel, Uga, and Sonny—all three in black tie (see p. 76)—was featured in major newspapers around the country. Uga IV was heralded as the only mascot to attend a Heisman dinner, and the photo made it into Chevy Chase's "Weekend Update" segment on *Saturday Night Live.*

Uga IV's Heisman distinction would ultimately land him in *Dog Fancy* magazine's "100 Great Dog Moments of the Century," along with Rin Tin Tin's film debut, Tramp romancing Lady, and Laika being launched into space aboard Sputnik 2. Uga IV added to his list of firsts a few months later when he and Charles traveled to Albuquerque for Georgia's Final Four appearance at the '83 NCAA basketball tournament—another first for the Georgia mascot.

When the Georgia basketball team made it to the 1983 Final Four in Albuquerque, Uga IV was there to cheer 'em on!

Uga IV and Sonny in the pages of *Midnight*

When author John Berendt was researching *Midnight in the Garden of Good and Evil* during the 1980s, one of the principal characters in his best-selling nonfiction book was Sonny Seiler, who got accused murderer Jim Williams acquitted in the longest murder trial in Georgia history. Berendt became a good friend of Sonny's, who was the lead attorney for all except the first of a four-trial legal marathon.

To know Sonny is to know his dog and his alma mater. During the second trial, Berendt became fascinated with Seiler's allegiance to the University of Georgia and his trips to football games with Uga IV. At one point, Jim Williams was even concerned that Sonny's Georgia football duties might distract his attention from the case.

No way, said Sonny, who invited Berendt to Athens to see what all the hoopla was about.

"I told Berendt, 'You ought to see at least one game. Come by our hotel suite beforehand. We always have a little gathering—and that's when Uga gets dressed.'"

Berendt came to Athens for Georgia's '83 season-opener against UCLA. He showed up at the Georgia Center and was directed to Sonny's suite, where the Seilers' traditional pregame party was in full swing. Sonny, Swann, Charles, and Uga IV were entertaining regular guests Harry Middleton, Bobby Lenihan, Herb Watkins, John Brim, Ken Hansing, Ty Butler, and a steady stream of drop-ins who came by to pay their respects and pat Uga IV on the head for good luck.

Uga IV

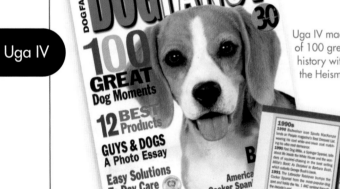

Uga IV made *Dog Fancy*'s list of 100 great moments in dog history with his 1982 trip to the Heisman Trophy banquet.

Berendt was particularly interested in the so-called "dressing of the dog," which he chronicled in detail in chapter twenty of "The Book," as it's referred to in Savannah. On page 275 of *Midnight*, Swann Seiler says, "Daddy, it's time to dress Uga." The next sentence reads, "'Ah, the Dressing of the Dog!'" intoned a portly man standing by the window."

"Now that *Midnight* is so famous," says Sonny, "both Ty Butler and Ken Hansing claim to have been the portly man standing by the window—and in truth, either one of them could've qualified!"

"The dressing of the dog always draws a crowd," says Sonny, who likes to have a number of Uga jerseys on hand to accommodate both his superstitions and changes in game temperature. If Georgia plays well in a certain jersey or pulls out a big win, Sonny will keep Uga in that jersey until it loses its magic. "If we play poorly or lose a big game," says Sonny, "I'll send that jersey to the outer limits of hell!"

At one point in the *Midnight* case, accused murderer Jim Williams expressed concern that Sonny Seiler—who was his defense attorney—might be distracted by his allegiance to Georgia football. Sonny assured Williams he was in good hands, eventually winning the case. To capture the flavor of Georgia football, *Midnight* author John Berendt visited Athens on game day to see Uga and the Bulldogs in action. Berendt included details of the "Dressing of the Dog" in chapter twenty of his record-breaking bestseller.

Return visit to the Capitol

So all-encompassing is the reach and reputation of the Georgia mascots that, when one has made an appearance in the state house chambers, you can bet it won't be long till the state senate demands equal time.

In January 1981, Uga III had led a procession through the house chambers in honor of the 1980 National Championship team. In February 1984, his son, Uga IV, matched his famous father by leading the '83 Georgia team, coaches, and cheerleaders through the state senate chambers.

To show their appreciation for the 10-1-1 Bulldogs, who had upset second-ranked Texas 10-9 on New Year's Day in the Cotton Bowl, the lawmakers passed five resolutions honoring the team.

Swann and Sonny with Uga IV at the 1984 Cotton Bowl, where quarterback John Lastinger's 17-yard touchdown run with 3:22 to go in the game enabled Georgia to upset second-ranked Texas 10-9.

But that's not to say that they dropped all legislative matters the moment Uga passed through the chamber doors. After a brief visit to the state house, where he got his head patted a few dozen times, Uga IV paced back and forth at the rear of the senate chambers as UGA alumnus Pierre Howard gave a twenty-minute speech on an employment bill. When Howard finished, it was Uga's turn.

"How 'bout that bulldog!" one senator shouted as Uga strutted down the aisle and plopped down next to another UGA alumnus, then-Lieutenant Governor Zell Miller. From there, it was on to the office of yet another alum—Governor Joe Frank Harris—where Sonny Seiler, at the invitation of the governor, boosted Uga IV onto Governor Harris' desk for a group photo.

"Knowing the kind of Georgia booster the governor is, I think Uga's visit was a pretty big deal," says Sonny. "But to Uga, it was just another day in the limelight."

Chair dog for "Great American Smokeout"

In 1984, the American Cancer Society decided to conduct a nationwide drive to encourage Americans to quit smoking. To get the public's attention, the cancer society asked the University of Georgia if Uga IV could serve as national "Chair-Dog" for the "Great American Smokeout."

"Uga IV was selected because of his national prominence, his reputation as a winner, and because he was an inspiration to young people," says Sonny. "In his capacity as Chair-Dog, he made numerous public appearances and was actually 'quoted' in American Cancer Society literature as to the dangers of smoking."

At the close of the "Great American Smokeout" campaign, the ACS presented Uga IV with an honorary plaque, which still hangs in the Seilers' den as a reminder of what he did for this worthy cause.

Uga IV

To show their appreciation for the 10-1-1 Bulldogs, who had upset second-ranked Texas 10-9 on New Year's Day in the Cotton Bowl, Governor Joe Frank Harris and state lawmakers honored the team, coaches, cheerleaders—and Uga IV—at the Capitol. Afterward, Sonny and Uga posed for a private photo with the governor.

Uga IV

[THEY SAID IT]

"He had a splendid voice that rumbled forth basso profundo when he addressed large conventions, a talent that might make Georgia president Charles Knapp envious. That and the fact that the Ugas rate one more page than Knapp does in the *Bulldog Media Guide.*

—Franz Lidz, *Sports Illustrated*

The Little Bulldog

by
Mimi Skandalakis

Illustrated by
Jan Matthews
and
Polly Neal

In 1985, UGA's University Woman's Club raised money for its First Ladies Scholarship Fund by publishing a children's book, *The Little Bulldog*. The limited press run edition was loosely based on the story of how Uga I became Georgia's mascot.

Bad wheels

A little-known fact about English bulldogs is that they love to run. They may be built low to the ground, but—like Verron Haynes—they will fool you with their straight-ahead speed and ability to cut.

"Distance is not their forte," says Sonny, "but, believe it or not, for the first 50 yards, an English bulldog can outrun a race-horse. Uga IV was no exception. He loved to run."

In April 1986, a few days before Georgia's G-Day intrasquad game in Athens, Uga IV was running around the Seilers' back-yard in Savannah. By Saturday morning before the G-day game, he had developed a limp in his right hind leg.

"We thought for awhile that it was just a thorn in the pad of his foot," says Sonny, "but we couldn't find anything and he continued to limp. After the G-day game, we took him to the UGA vet school for X-rays. They found he had torn the cruciate ligament in his right rear knee, the same kind of injury athletes suffer, oftentimes when they're hit making a cut while running. Apparently, Uga IV injured himself while running in our back-yard. The doctors concluded that, unless he had surgery, he would develop advanced arthritis and could be permanently lame."

Uga IV

It was fortunate that Uga IV's injury and subsequent surgery occurred during the off-season. He wore a hard cast for four weeks and then a soft cast for another week and a half before he was allowed to leave the vet school and return to Savannah.

"We thought our problems were over," says Sonny, "but during examinations at the vet school they found that Uga IV also suffered from dry eye—the same condition that had given Uga III so much trouble, though not as bad. We treated it with artificial tears and a special eye ointment that had to be applied once a day."

The Seiler family posed in the backyard of their Dutch Island home for the cover of the September 20, 1986, game program. The story included a photo of Uga IV at poolside.

Sonny and Uga IV on the dock at Dutch Island. The mascots can be trusted to be well-behaved in any environment—from a fishing boat in South Georgia to a black-tie banquet in Manhattan—but they aren't perfect. "Have they occasionally acted like an ordinary dog and done something they shouldn't have? Yes!" says Sonny. "But I'm amazed it hasn't happened more often."

Trouble with wheelbarrows

"Talking about how Uga IV loved to run reminds me of an incident with the red wheelbarrow that we used for lawn work," says Sonny. "When Uga IV was a puppy, he enjoyed being pushed in that wheelbarrow. He got so attached to it that he would charge it if you tried to use it for yard work when he was outside. He'd get so excited he would actually attack the wheel barrow and bite it with his teeth."

The Seilers eventually quit using their red wheelbarrow because of Uga IV's peculiarities. One day, a crew of lawn men were working in the backyard at the Seilers' home on Dutch Island—and one of them grabbed the red wheelbarrow and started pushing it across the back lawn to a truck. Uga IV, who had been watching with interest from the back porch, took off like a bull after a matador. He hit the red wheelbarrow on the dead run and turned it over. It frightened one of the workers so badly that he took off for the truck.

"We had a hell of a time convincing him that Uga wasn't really after him—he just liked the wheelbarrow," says Sonny. "Swann said it best when she told a sports reporter, 'He's like Don Quixote tilting at windmills.'"

Uga IV

Halfway through the 1986 season, Uga IV jumped off the bed at the Georgia Center and tore the cruciate ligament in his left rear leg.

Introducing . . . Otto, the super sub

The Substitute
To fate resigned, he waits upon the bench
And leans his chin upon his hands,
He watches every play and vaguely hears
The cheers that thunder from the stand.
Out there his teammates execute the plays
His sweat and toil help them to learn,
While he, a sub, can only watch and hope
And patiently await his turn.
The din of cheering crowds rolls o'er his head
Unknown the service he performs,
They only see him waiting for his chance
The chance that often never comes.
Unsung, but still alert to give his best
Content when thousands laud his mates,
Successful teams were never built
Without the sub, who hopes, and works and waits.

—Grantland Rice

Halfway through the 1986 season, Uga IV was injured again. It happened the morning of the Vanderbilt game.

"He was in a rambunctious and playful mood, and he just rolled off the bed at the Georgia Center," says Sonny. "He didn't act like he was in pain, so we took him to the game—and he gutted it out. But by the third quarter he was unable to walk. I had to carry him off the field."

Georgia's team orthopedist Butch Mulherin took a look at Uga IV's injury right there at Sanford Stadium, and made an instant diagnosis.

"I'm sorry, Sonny," said Dr. Mulherin, "but Uga has torn the cruciate ligament in his left rear leg. He's going to need surgery."

Mulherin's diagnosis was confirmed by Dr. Robert Basinger at the vet school later that afternoon.

"Bulldogs are built a lot like football players," says Dr. Bruce Hollett of the UGA vet school. "They have wide shoul-

Pressed into service when his brother, Uga IV, was injured in '86, Otto certainly looked the part . . . except for the large brown-and-black spot that is visible in both this portrait and in the backyard shot with Sonny and Uga IV. That's Otto on the right.

Uga IV

ders, a well-developed chest, and narrow hips—which is why most bulldog puppies have to be delivered by Cesarean section. And, like football players, they're vulnerable to knee injuries."

While Uga IV was recovering from surgery, performed by Dr. Dennis Aron of the vet school, it was up to his seven-year-old brother Otto to step in and finish the 1986 season.

"Otto was mostly white and he had a great head," says Sonny, "but we didn't think of him as mascot material because he had a large brown-and-black spot on his back that ran down his hindquarters to his tail. Uga I, II, and Otto's father, Uga III, were all white—and we wanted to maintain that tradition. Otto was a sweet dog, who had simply hung out at our house eating and sleeping until we needed him."

Uga IV's injury continued a string of bad luck for the Georgia football program.

"It's great to know we have strength in reserve with our dogs— something we don't have with our team," said Vince Dooley, who had just lost his top two running backs, Tim Worley and Keith Henderson, to knee injuries. "I know Otto personally, and he's a fine dog. I visited them both this summer, and it's hard to tell which is which. He'll be a first-line substitute for Uga."

Georgia was fortunate to have an Otto waiting in the wings, as opposed to the situation over at Auburn, where War Eagle V had died unexpectedly in September 1986 and there was no heir apparent to take his place.

Otto, on the other hand, had been waiting for his chance for years.

"He has no, absolutely no, game experience," sports information director Claude Felton told reporters, "but Sonny Seiler assures me that he's been studying Uga IV's playbook."

All kidding aside, it's not an easy task for a family pet to suddenly be thrust into service in front of 82,000 cheering fans. But Otto handled his game-day chores with relative ease and the Sanford Stadium fans warmed to him immediately.

The Georgia team posted easy victories in Otto's first two games, against Kentucky and Richmond, and when he trotted out onto the field for the Florida game in Jacksonville, the Georgia half of the Gator Bowl erupted with the chant, "Two and 0 with Otto! Two and 0 with Otto!" Georgia lost to Florida that day 31-19, but then upset Auburn on the road 20-16. That was the infamous game where Auburn security officials turned sprinklers on Georgia fans for celebrating on the field after the game.

During his three-week stay at the UGA vet school, Uga IV received more than 100 get-well items and presents—cards, telegrams, letters, flower arrangements, balloons, bones, and doggie treats—including a get-well card from Kentucky's wildcat mascot.

Tim Worley, who was out for the season with a knee injury, received only about a dozen get-well cards.

"Uga's got that beat paws down," said his veterinarian, Dr. Aron.

The Seilers didn't want to take any chances with Uga IV's leg after it was operated on, so he sat out several games. Like a quarterback who wears a special jersey at practice so he won't be hit, Uga IV wore a white T-shirt with a red cross on the back to indicate he was still on the disabled list. Outfitted with a soft cast, he and Otto tag-teamed the '86 Georgia Tech game, which Georgia won 31-24. Uga IV was back at full strength for Georgia's 27-24 Bluebonnet Bowl loss to Boston College.

Uga IV

When Georgia's star running back Tim Worley suffered a season-ending knee injury in 1986, he received only about a dozen get-well cards. Uga IV had more than that taped to his pen at the vet school. During his three-week stay, Uga IV received more than 100 cards, get-well wishes, and presents.

Like a quarterback on injured reserve, Uga IV wore a Red Cross shirt to indicate he was on the disabled list after surgery on his injured leg. Outfitted with a soft cast, he tangled with Tech's mascot in the '86 regular-season finale.

Uga IV

The relationship between the mascots and Vince Dooley (shown here being carried off the field after his final game as head coach in 1988) dates back to Dooley's hiring in 1964 during Uga I's tenure. As athletic director, he has presided over the dogs' funerals, and he has a soft spot in his heart for Otto, the sub who provided "bench strength."

Otto's brief tour of duty ended with a 4-1 record. In June 1989, he developed swelling in his legs, which prevented him from walking. The Seilers took him to their Savannah vet, where, on Sunday, July 7, 1989, Otto suffered a fatal heart attack. Newspapers all over the country carried the news of his death.

"We're saddened to lose Otto," said Dooley, "but he did have his day in the sun. He will be remembered for generations to come because he stepped forward at a critical time and performed like a champion when we needed him."

"Coach Dooley showed such appreciation for Otto," says Sonny, "that I suspect Otto is actually his favorite mascot. He often referred to Otto as 'bench strength.' We're just glad Otto was around to fill in. I don't think he ever expected anything more out of life than just being a pet, and we loved him irrespective of him having to fill in as mascot. He was as popular in our family as Uga IV."

Otto didn't qualify for burial in Sanford Stadium, but loving hands laid him to rest in the Seilers' backyard on Dutch Island. His resting place was marked by a plum tree that bore delicious

fruit. Otto's grave has since been moved to the Seilers' new home near the Savannah Yacht Club. The white marble gravestone is engraved with Coach Dooley's quote:

OTTO DFB
1978–1989
Son of Uga III
Brother of Uga IV
"He had his day in the sun and performed like a
champion when we needed him. . . ."

—Vince Dooley

When Otto died, the Seilers laid him to rest in their backyard on Dutch Island. His grave has since been moved to their new home near the Savannah Yacht Club. The initials "DFB" on his gravestone stand for Otto's nickname: Dog-faced boy.

Uga IV contributes to medical research

By the summer of 1987, Uga IV's knees had fully healed and he was walking without any noticeable limp. But the dry eye problem that had cropped up in 1986 persisted. The Seilers noticed changes in Uga's left eye, and the condition would no longer respond to traditional medication.

Fortunately, Dr. Renee Kaswan, professor of veterinary opthalmology and pharmacology at the UGA vet school, had been experimenting with cyclosporine—a drug used to prevent organ rejection in human transplant patients—as a treatment for animals with eye problems. Dr. Kaswan had been working with Dr. John Williamson, a senior consultant in opthalmology at Southern General Hospital. Dr. Williamson had been treating twenty patients suffering from dry eye, and they had shown improvement with cyclosporine therapy.

In July, with Uga IV at risk for corneal ulcers—even blindness—Dr. Kaswan started him on a two-percent cyclosporine solution. He was one of only four dogs in the country to undergo the experimental treatment. Seven weeks later, Uga IV's eye was no longer inflamed and there was a notable increase in tear flow.

Uga IV

The only time Uga wears green is for Savannah's much-ballyhooed St. Patrick's Day parade.

Years later, a 1998 issue of the *Medical Tribune* used a photo of Uga IV to illustrate a feature story on Dr. Kaswan. The layout included medical photos of Uga's left eye before and after cyclosporine treatment. The comparison was extraordinary; tear production increased, and through continued use of the drug—

under the care of Dr. Kaswan and her UGA colleague, Dr. Victoria Pentlarge—Uga IV's sight was saved and no surgery was necessary.

In Uga IV's medical records, Dr. Kaswan made the following entry: "Uga is the ultimate test animal."

Through the experiment with Uga IV and continued research with cyclosporine, Dr. Kaswan gained national recognition for her work. After eighteen months of therapy with cyclosporine, Uga's dry eye condition was completely controlled and, shortly thereafter, the Food and Drug Administration approved ophthalmic cyclosporine for the treatment of dry eye in humans.

The great Lillie hoax

Loran Smith has worn many hats at the University of Georgia, from his days as captain of the track team to his tenure as secretary of the Bulldog Club to his pre-game, post-game, and sideline reporter duties on the Georgia Radio Network. What some people may not know is that Smith is also a great practical joker! And in the fall of 1988, he decided to take on Sonny and Uga IV.

"Get the picture," says Sonny. "This was the era of Women's Lib, and Title IX was beginning to have a dramatic effect on men's and women's programs in intercollegiate athletics. Fortunately, UGA's academic and athletic leadership had anticipated the financial repercussions of Title IX and we were way ahead of most Division I schools in providing better facilities and increased opportunities for women athletes."

It was Georgia's well-established fan base for women's athletics that gave Loran Smith the idea for his practical joke. The scheme began with a bogus letter that Smith addressed to athletic director Vince Dooley. Posing as real-life alumnus Gus Johnson from Winder—who was in on the joke, as was Dooley—Smith wrote that it was time for Georgia's women's athletic program to have its own bulldog mascot. The letter suggested that Uga IV, although a dedicated standard-bearer, could not easily travel the distance from Savannah to Athens to appear at both men's and women's events. The letter went on to say that Johnson's female bulldog, Lillie, could represent women's sports and serve as a backup mascot to Uga IV.

The letter described Lillie as "a great female dog with a high-pitched voice who has been taught to bark on command and thereby gain attention at the games. She has a dark brown spot around her left eye and a dark brown spot on her tail, but she's all bulldog. She really looks cute, especially when we dress her in female attire for the games."

Smith came close to overplaying his hand with that last part, but when he forwarded the letter to Sonny in Savannah he attached a bogus memo typed on Dooley's personal stationery that read: "Loran—he makes some good points—check with Sonny and get back to me on this—Vince."

"Needless to say, I was both puzzled and concerned," says Sonny. "Puzzled because we had never refused to take Uga to any women's' athletic event to which he was invited. And concerned because I was a close friend of women's athletic director Liz Murphy and she had never indicated any desire to tamper with Georgia's long-standing mascot tradition."

An expert at preparing legal briefs, Sonny took the letter seriously enough to put together an eight-page response for Dooley in which he cited all the reasons why it would be unwise and impractical to have more than one bulldog mascot. Instead of mailing it, Sonny decided to hand carry it to Athens and give it to Dooley in person the following week.

Smith had gotten two of Sonny's close friends, Johnny Peters Jr. and Remer Lane, both of Savannah, involved in the charade. Peters even went to the trouble and expense of having an oil portrait done of the fictitious female bulldog Lillie.

"The longer the thing went on, the more convinced I was that it was a hoax—but I thought it would be fun to play along," says Sonny, who was invited to Remer Lane's home one evening, along with a number of other Georgia alums.

"The purpose of the get-together was the unveiling of the painting," says Sonny, "but I knew it would also involve the unmasking of the practical jokers."

The conspirators were quick to admit the truth, and the painting—which showed Lillie wearing lipstick and earrings in a short skirt and halter top—delighted the party guests. Sonny got a good laugh out of it, and he made a place for the Lillie portrait amongst all the other Uga paraphernalia that he and his family have collected over the years.

"I later met and shared a laugh with Gus Johnson of Winder," says Sonny. "Have I gotten Loran Smith back? No, not yet . . . but I promise you, he's always looking over his shoulder."

Uga IV

Lillie, a fictitious female mascot for Georgia's women's sports teams, was a practical joke hatched by Bulldog Club secretary and radio network sideline reporter Loran Smith. That's Smith at right in the photo at left, as Sonny tells the Lillie tale to former Georgia and NFL great Fran Tarkenton.

Uga IV

"People pet him so much his head gets sore. He's like a politician who shakes too many hands."

—Sonny Seiler

A family favorite

Uga IV occupies a special place in the hearts of the Seiler family for a number of reasons. For starters, he was the first dog since Uga I to live exclusively indoors. The family spent less time with II and III because they lived in a special area Sonny created for them in the garage. To make sure they were comfy during Savannah's short winters, Sonny cut a hole in the laundry room wall so a sixty-gallon water heater would warm one of the garage walls. The dogs would cozy up to that wall and stay warm at night.

Uga IV was the first of the dogs to sleep in the kitchen.

"I think he's probably Mama's favorite," says Charles. "Uga III died while I was off at college and Swann had a place of her own, so having Uga IV there to keep her company was important to her at that time."

Cecelia has her own way of remembering Uga IV.

"All of our dogs have been wonderful," she says, "but IV was probably the best-looking and the sweetest."

Sonny remembers him as the most personable and cooperative, volunteering his paw on those rare occasions when Sonny wanted to create a paw-print autograph.

Swann remembers Uga IV as the most playful.

"Charles and I played 'Mad Dog' games with Uga IV," she recalls. "He'd chase us from room to room, and if you got in his way he'd tackle you. If you swung a wet towel in the air, he'd get so riled up he'd grab it and shake water all over the room. If he saw a cooler of ice, he'd bang into it just for fun."

Occasionally, a hotel employee unfamiliar with Uga IV's penchant for playtime would need assistance.

"I remember coming back to our room at the Le Méridien Hotel in New Orleans," says Swann, "and finding that Uga IV had backed an unsuspecting maid all the way into the bathroom. By the time we got there, she was standing on the toilet. She probably thought her life was in jeopardy, but Uga was just having fun!"

There's another reason that Swann has a soft spot in her heart for Uga IV: he was staying with her when he died.

Uga IV

> December 3, 1985
>
> Dear Coach Marolt:
>
>   Coach Vince Dooley has referred your kind invitation to Chip's Invitational Mascot Ski Race to my owner, Frank Seiler of Savannah.
>
>   Barring any unforseen complications, my "brother," Charles Seiler is planning to accompany me to this event to represent the University of Georgia. Although there is not much snow here in Savannah, Charles is a good skier, and I am a fast learner -- although I lack Chip's experience.
>
>   We are mailing the invitation form to Ms. Pat Peeples as requested in your letter. My owner Frank "Sonny" Seiler looks forward to receiving additional information on this event.
>
>   Mr. Claude Felton, our Sports Information Director will be glad to provide any requested information about our program.
>
>   Look forward to seeing you in April.
>
>   Kindest regards,
>
>   UGA IV

A family favorite because he was so personable and playful, Uga IV even had his own stationery, which he used to respond to invitations. When you saw the paw print, you knew it came from the genuine article.

Farewell to Uga IV

In 1989, near the end of Uga IV's ninth season as mascot, the Seilers noticed a change in his eating habits. He began losing weight, his energy level was down, his movements were noticeably slower, and by December his facial features also began to change.

"We took Uga IV to our local vet, who discovered fluid in his lungs," Sonny recalls. "So we took him to the UGA vet school, where they did a sonogram and discovered three growths. A biopsy revealed that he had cancer. When bulldogs get cancer, they usually go downhill fast."

Medication kept Uga IV comfortable, but his illness prevented him from attending the '89 Peach Bowl in Atlanta.

"Uga IV had sired several all-white pups over the years," says Sonny, "and one of them, Magillicuddy I, filled in for him admirably at the Peach Bowl."

On Sunday, February 25, 1990, Uga IV sat with his family as they watched the Georgia-LSU basketball game on TV. A

Neville Austin free throw with four seconds left gave the Dogs an 86-85 victory and a share of first place in the SEC. Sonny and Cecelia went out of town on Monday, so Uga IV was staying at Swann's townhouse in downtown Savannah.

"I remember hearing that God picks who's with you when you pass away, and I'm happy he picked me to be with Uga IV," says Swann, who still gets emotional talking about it years later. "He was resting in the sun on my back porch when I went out to see how he was doing. When I sat down next to him, he gave one last sigh—and then slumped against me, like he'd been waiting for me to come out and say goodbye to him."

Uga IV had served nine seasons and his teams had gone to nine bowl games—a record that still stands. Athletic director Vince Dooley called Uga IV "The Dog of the Decade"—and that became his epitaph.

On the day following Uga IV's death, February 28, 1990, Sonny and son Charles took him on his final trip to Athens. At noon, a private burial was held at Sanford Stadium, where Uga IV's three forefathers were already at rest. The rest of the Seiler family arrived in separate cars. Also in attendance were Vince Dooley, UGA president Charles Knapp, former tennis coach Dan Magill, and a number of friends from the University and Athens communities. "I looked up on the bridge, and it was just packed with students," Swann recalls. "You could've heard a pin drop . . . until they saw that little red-and-black wooden coffin, and then you could hear a quiet murmur moving through the crowd."

Cards and letters poured in from all over the country following Uga IV's death. Swann's good friend Debra Norville, who had participated in the pink pooch caper with Uga III (see p. 54), paid tribute to Uga IV on NBC's *Today Show.* ESPN and CNN also mentioned his passing. State Representative Charles Poag authored a resolution that paid tribute to Uga IV. It ended with these words:

"Although he is gone from us now, our much-loved Uga IV will live on forever in the hearts and souls of Bulldawg students, alumni, players, and fans everywhere who honor and revere his memory."

Uga IV

Sonny speaks with a group of people that included UGA president Charles Knapp and Vince Dooley prior to Uga IV's funeral on February 28, 1990. The grave site had been renovated six months earlier to reinforce and expand the retaining wall.

Dr. Robert Hirshberg, D.V.M.,
who served as head cheerleader at UGA in the 1950s,
penned the following poem:

UGA IV

Here's to Uga, he was my friend,
I know in heaven we'll meet again,
Although we hate that he's deceased,
Please take him Lord and give him peace.

All dogs go to heaven, so they say,
And Uga never asked for any pay,
A friendly pat on his head,
On the field or in his bed,
The best of Bulldogs has received his call,
But we will miss him in the fall.

Yes, he'll be missed when our reunion starts,
at homecoming when with all our hearts,
The Alumni Cheerleaders will always yell,
And after the game ring the Chapel Bell.

Rings for Victory and in this case,
A certain Bulldog will set the pace,
We praise our Uga we loved his face,
So Lord please honor our last request,
Make our beloved mascot Uga your honored guest.

Uga IV

UGA IV

GEORGIA MASCOT
1981-1990
TWO S.E.C. CHAMPIONSHIPS
NINE BOWL TEAMS
HEISMAN TROPHY BANQUET
NEW YORK CITY 1982
N.C.A.A. FINAL FOUR 1983
S.E.C. BASKETBALL
CHAMPIONSHIP 1990
"THE DOG OF THE DECADE"

"UGA"
THE REAL GEORGIA BULLDOG...
WHOSE COURAGE, LOYALTY AND
DETERMINATION EXEMPLIFIES
THE SPIRIT OF THE TEAMS
HE REPRESENTS.
THESE BULLDOG
AND PR

Uga V
1990–99

Born
March 6, 1990

AKC registered name
Uga IV's Magillicuddy II

Dates of service
September 8, 1990
to September 11, 1999

Football record
65-39-1

Bowl record
4-1

beat Arkansas 24-15
in '91 Independence Bowl

beat Ohio State 21-14
in '93 Citrus Bowl

lost to Virginia 34-27
in '95 Peach Bowl

beat Wisconsin 33-6
in '98 Outback Bowl

beat Virginia 35-33
in '98 Peach Bowl

Died
November 22, 1999

Epitaph
"Defender of his Turf"

Uga V

The Mascot Who Became a Celebrity

Unlike his son, Uga III, who entered the final stages of his tenure without having sired a suitable heir, Uga IV had produced several all-white puppies who could have become Uga V if the fates had been different. But Uga IV's tenure encompassed nine seasons and by the time he contracted cancer in 1989, the next all-white heir in line was no longer a puppy.

"With all the physical demands on these dogs," says Sonny, "I was looking for a true freshman—a young dog bursting with energy, as all the mascots have been when they first donned the spiked collar. But I wasn't sure that was possible with Uga IV on his last legs."

A phone call out of the blue got the mascot line started back in 1956, and it happened again with the birth of Uga V.

Named for Georgia's hall of fame tennis coach and long-time sports information director Dan Magill, who anointed Uga I back in 1956, Magillicudy II started out as a mascot but, as Uga V, he became a celebrity.

One of the most difficult aspects of maintaining the mascot line over nearly a half-century has been making sure there is an all-white puppy in reserve at all times. Uga IV served so long that this all-white heir, Magillicuddy I, never got the call—except as a one-game substitute for his sick father at the 1989 Peach Bowl.

Uga V

The call came from friends in South Carolina who wanted to arrange a date between their English bulldog and Uga IV. Ordinarily, the Seilers initiate such matters, breeding the mascot approximately twice a year—but never during football season and always in consultation with reproductive and genetic experts at the UGA College of Veterinary Medicine. Given Uga IV's deteriorating health, the Seilers decided they had nothing to lose.

"The vet said he wasn't sure if there was any spark left in Uga IV, but we got them together on a Friday," Sonny recalls. "On Saturday, the vet called and said, 'Sonny, you better come and get Uga. This is too taxing on him. He mated one time and it took a lot out of him. He's having some trouble breathing.'"

Game over, Sonny figured. But eleven days after Uga IV died, the Seilers learned that his final companion was expecting.

On birthing day, March 6, 1990, with the Seilers waiting in nervous anticipation down in Savannah, the first pup to emerge was . . . brown and white. The second pup was . . . white . . . but with a brown spot on his tail. Ten minutes passed and then the third pup—and, as it turned out, the last one in the litter—began to emerge. He was . . . male . . . and . . . a little snowball, pure as ivory!

"We were ecstatic!" says Sonny. "The combination of this little pup's good looks and the age of his uncles made Magillicuddy II the fifth in the proud line of bulldog mascots."

Named for Georgia's long-time tennis coach and sports information director Dan Magill, who had, in effect, anointed Uga I back in 1956, little Magillicuddy II may have come in like a mascot but, as Uga V, he went out like a celebrity.

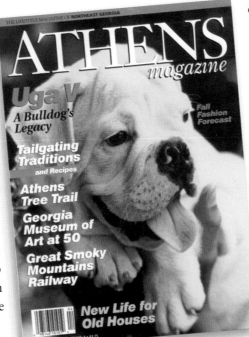

English bulldogs catch a lot of grief over their looks, but as puppies they're adorable.

A box of Uga V photos yielded these two golden oldies: the time it snowed on Dutch Island and Uga V getting a hug from someone in a floppy hat. Can you guess the identity of this man, whose Athens home is a veritable Bulldog museum? See Chapter 6.

Uga V

[THEY SAID IT]

"A SORT OF MODERN-DAY CHAPLIN, Uga [V] is more expressive in pictures than words. He has rarely been heard by anyone outside his immediate family and doesn't discuss his current popularity surge. In fact, he dismisses most questions with a sort of slobbering gurgle that could be duplicated by sucking Jell-O through a garbage disposal."

—Timothy Guidera,
Savannah Morning News

Uga V (shown here with big sisters Sara and Bess Seiler) was just six months old when he made his home debut on September 15, 1990. He was so small that seamstress Nonie Sutton had to cut down a jersey Uga IV had worn in his debut in 1981.

Uga V

Baptism by fire: Baton Rouge on a Saturday night

Ray Goff was in his second season as head football coa Georgia when Uga V made his debut in Baton Rouge Saturday night—which is as hostile an environment as a foc team and a young mascot can encounter. Uga V had never be around Bayou-type crowds, excessive noise, or big-time colleg football games, but he got a dose of all three on the night of September 8, 1990. Just six months old, he was so small that Nonie Sutton had to cut down a jersey Uga IV had worn in his debut. Uga V handled the experience quite well, althoug Georgia got beat 18-13.

At a 1992 ceremony honoring Fran Tarkenton, former Georgia great Bill Hartman tripped over Uga V and ended up on the Sanford Stadium turf. Were people worried that the Bulldog hall of famer and kicking coach had injured himself? No way, says Hartman: "85,000 people thought I'd killed Uga!"

Uga V made his home debut a week later at Sanford Stadium, where he was greeted with a standing ovation and cries of "Damn Good Dog! . . . Damn Good Dog! . . . Damn Good Dog!" from a game-day crowd that never got to say goodbye to Uga IV. Fortunately, the outcome was better than in Baton Rouge, as Georgia edged upset-minded Southern Mississippi 18-17—and that got Uga V's whirlwind reign off and running.

Bulldog sculptures heighten school spirit

Two important additions to Sanford Stadium were unveiled on September 11, 1992. The first was a two-ton granite statue of a bulldog that was created by Atlanta sculptor Steve Mooney and presented to the university as a gift from the Elberton (Georgia) Bulldog Club. The project was conceived by Tom Oglesby, owner of Keystone Memorials, and it became an instant favorite with Georgia players, who give the granite bulldog a pat for good luck as they run onto the field.

"Just as Michelangelo freed David, Steve Mooney looked into this huge block of granite and knew he had to free the bulldog," said Vince Dooley at the unveiling. "We put him in the end zone because he has a nose for the goal line on offense. And don't be surprised if Coach Goff calls on him to play some defense as well."

Mooney used photos of the mascots to give the sculpture its unique look. "I wanted to capture the character of the dog and the essence of the Georgia Bulldogs," he says. "I looked at these dogs very closely before working on the details." A crane was required to lift the 4,820-pound sculpture over the walls of Sanford Stadium and onto its pedestal behind the east end zone.

The second addition was a bronze bulldog statue that watches over the mascots' graves at the southwest corner of Sanford Stadium. The project was initiated by 1943 UGA graduate

A tradition was born when Atlanta sculptor Steve Mooney's 4,820-pound granite sculpture was dedicated at the east end of Sanford Stadium on September 11, 1992. Georgia players always "pet the dog" as they take the field prior to every home game.

Uga V

101

Columbus, Georgia, sculptor and portrait artist Wyndell Taylor's bronze rendering of Uga—which stands guard over the mascots' graves at the southwest corner of Sanford Stadium—has inspired the fans' version of "pet the dog." As people file into the stadium, many of them stop to pet the bronze statue for good luck.

Uga V

Richard Hecht, a Columbus, Georgia, resident who said he wanted to recognize both the Seiler family and the line of Uga mascots because "I believe they are responsible for the intense loyalty and enthusiasm people have for the University of Georgia."

With help from the UGA Bulldog Club, Hecht raised enough money to commission Columbus sculptor and portrait artist Wyndell Taylor to create a life-size bronze rendering of Uga that has inspired the fans' version of "pet the dog." When the Georgia players run out onto the field prior to every home game, they pet Steve Mooney's granite bulldog for good luck. And as Georgia fans file into Sanford Stadium, many of them stop to pet Wyndell Taylor's bronze Uga for good luck.

Uga V made the cover of the 1993 year-end issue of *Dog* magazine, which named him "Favorite Dog of the Year."

Uga V is first member of National Alumni Association

The University of Georgia National Alumni Association was established in 1995, and Sonny Seiler was tapped as its first president. The independent, dues-based organization was created to be the official representative and rallying point for UGA's 200,000 living alumni—which raised an important question: who should be the first member of the newly christened NAA?

Answer: Uga V.

Dave Muia, director of alumni relations at the University of Georgia, made the proposal to the NAA officers and board of directors. The vote was unanimous, and, nearly forty years after his great-great-grandfather was issued a student ID card, Uga V was issued membership card No. 1 in the National Alumni Association. He signed it himself with Cecelia helping him affix his paw print. Uga V attended the first official meeting of the association and has been since used as the poster dog for national membership campaigns.

Uga V

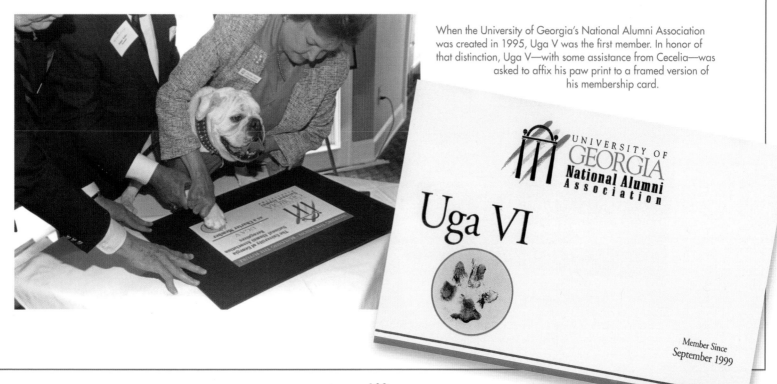

When the University of Georgia's National Alumni Association was created in 1995, Uga V was the first member. In honor of that distinction, Uga V—with some assistance from Cecelia—was asked to affix his paw print to a framed version of his membership card.

UNIVERSITY OF
GEORGIA
National Alumni
Association

Uga VI

Member Since
September 1999

Uga, the ad dog

In the midst of the Herschel Walker era, the UGA Athletic Association realized that sports memorabilia was becoming a big business. Georgia logos and slogans were appearing on everything from T-shirts to ashtrays to book covers, and the university wasn't seeing any of that revenue. Vince Dooley was aware that the University of Michigan had already taken steps to copyright its memorabilia to protect the use of the school's slogans and participate in profits from the sale of such products and material.

To capitalize on its marketing potential, the UGA athletic board approved the hiring of promotions director Avery McLean, who oversaw the process by which Georgia legally protected its slogans, logos, trademarks, and memorabilia. With the full cooperation of the Seilers, property rights were also established for the use of the mascot's name, his likeness, his appearances, and his endorsements.

In accordance with the Seilers' wishes, the university decided that the athletic department should be very selective in the use of the mascots for endorsements and commercials. Commercial use of Uga requires approval by the Seilers and by the athletic association, which is represented in such matters by the promotions director. An appropriate royalty is paid to the athletic association for the use of Uga's name, photo, and/or likeness.

"To their credit," says McLean, "the Seilers have always stayed in the background, conent for the university to receive the majority of glory and benefits."

Once these guidelines were in place, Uga became an even more popular subject for print and TV advertising.

Both Uga IV and Uga V endorsed Jim Dandy Dog Food, each dog posing for a poster that was used to advertise that product.

In 1989, Uga IV co-starred in Ray Goff's first TV commercial. The client was the Ford Motor Company, and the commercial showed first-year coach Goff and Uga IV riding in a Ford truck. What the TV audience couldn't see was Charlie Brannon, who was crouched on the floor of the truck holding Uga in perfect camera-ready position.

Uga V

Destined for the silver screen, Uga V got used to camera crews and bright lights as an advertising icon for commercial clients such as Cotton States, Arby's, and McDonald's (see p. 105). Both he and Uga VI have appeared in numerous institutional ads for the University of Georgia.

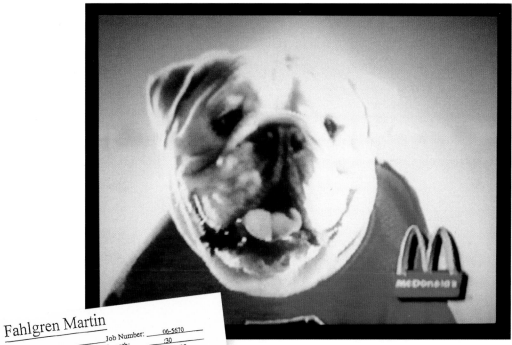

Fahlgren Martin

Job Number: 06-5670
Length: :30
Date: 8/10/93

Client: McDonald's
Product: RMCC Mini-Footballs
Title: "Real Mascots" (MCDMASC)

Audio:

Video:

OPEN ON ACTUAL BULLDOG SITTING IN LIMBO SET. HE HAS U-OF-G MINI-FOOTBALL NEARBY, AND IS PRETTY EXCITED, WAGGING TAIL, BREATHING HARD, ETC. FADE UP SMALL MCDONALD'S LOGO.

V/O: Hey Uga, see you got a mascot football from McDonald's.

COCA-COLA CLASSIC SLIDES ACROSS SCREEN. BULLDOG REACTS. SUPER: $2.99 WITH THE PURCHASE OF COCA-COLA CLASSIC. POP ON LOGOS: RONALD MCDONALD HOUSE, RMCC.

Just $2.99 with the purchase of any size Coca-Cola Classic. Part of the proceeds goes to help build the new Ronald McDonald House at Scottish Rite.

DISCLAIMER: At participating McDonald's. Price may vary. Plus tax. For a limited time.

G.T. FOOTBALL ROLLS IN. BULLDOG LOOKS AT IT AND GROWLS.

And did you know they also have Georgia Tech footballs?

(SFX OF BULLDOG WIMPERING.)

(SFX OF DOG GROWLING.)

CLOSE-UP OF BULLDOG BITING G.T. FOOTBALL.

CHOMP

(SFX OF UGA CHOPPING BALL, AIR FIZZING OUT.)

Didn't think so.

CAMERA PULLS BACK TO SHOW FLATTENED FOOTBALL WITH BULLDOG LOOKING SMUG.

Uga V posed for a Cotton States Insurance ad and for a Kodak "Capture the Moment" campaign that resulted in him being pictured on a giant poster that greeted visitors to Atlanta's Hartsfield Airport. In 1993, Sonny and Ceceilia took Uga V to Miami to appear in a TV spot for McDonald's. Hill's Pet Food contracted to use Uga V in the promotion of its Science Diet line in 1996, and Uga VI endorsed Prescription Diet Z/D for Hill's Pet Food in an ad brochure that was mailed to practicing veterinarians (see p. 34).

The Cotton States Insurance print ad shows Uga V with a torn-up football jersey in his mouth; the text reads: "About The Only Thing Cotton States Won't Insure Is The Visiting Team."

"That ad is so popular the company continues to run it in the Georgia football program years and years after we shot it," says Sonny. "But it wasn't easy getting Uga V to do what the photographer wanted him to do. You can't just snap your fingers and expect a dog to hold material in his mouth take after take."

But Sonny had an idea.

"Uga's crazy about bacon," he says, "so I wrapped some of it in the material, let him sniff it, and then put it in his mouth. I told the photographer, 'You better work fast because he'll have that bacon unwrapped and in his mouth in no time!'"

Uga V

Uga V

If it's a football Saturday, you can bet that a TV crew is aiming a camera at Uga.

Uga's star turn on ESPN

In August 1996, a film crew came to Athens to shoot a tongue-in-cheek, day-in-the-life feature on Uga that would serve as a lead-in to ESPN's fall football coverage.

Uga's storybook day opens with the Georgia football team finishing practice. A manager blows a whistle and says, "Everybody on the bus!" The noise awakens Uga V, who has been napping behind the tackling dummies, but as he shakes himself awake the team bus pulls away, leaving poor Uga V behind in a cloud of dusk. A heavy-hearted mascot then sets off to find his beloved Georgia players. He trudges along the railroad tracks, makes a brief pit stop at a fire hydrant, and finally locates the Georgia team at his master's old fraternity house—where his great-great grandfather got the mascot line started back in 1956. Recreating that historic day, Uga V races through a crowd of college students on the Sigma Chi lawn, bounds up the steps and into the frat house, where Sonny scoops him up and he finds the Georgia players sitting in front of a TV.

"Hey, Uga made it just in time!" they shout, and then the camera zooms in on the TV screen, where ESPN's college football coverage begins with images of Knute Rockne and Bear Bryant.

Truth did win out over fiction during the filming of the opening sequence when Uga V awakens from his nap.

"The first time they shot that part," says Sonny, "Uga chased the bus down and caught it. They had to re-shoot the entire scene, giving the bus a bigger head start!"

In all, more than fourteen hours of videotape were shot of Uga V. The edited feature was shown on the kickoff show and segments aired during ESPN's Thursday night *Weekend Kickoff* and Saturday *College Game Day* shows.

Signature moment No. 1: Uga defends his turf

The mascots have made many exciting trips to Auburn, Alabama, over the years, but the 100th meeting between the Deep South's oldest rivals added a remarkable new chapter to the Uga saga. The date was November 16, 1996, the Georgia-Auburn game was televised regionally by CBS, and no one in Jordan-Hare Stadium could have anticipated the fireworks that were about to transpire. Kickoff took place at 3:30 P.M. EST, the game lasted until well after dark, and CBS's instant replay crew got a workout from start to finish. Here's what happened:

With the game scoreless in the first quarter, Auburn quarterback Dameyune Craig lofted a 21-yard touchdown pass to receiver Robert Baker, who caught the ball in stride at the 2-yard line and scored. Baker's touchdown gave Auburn a 7-0 lead, but it will forever be overshadowed by his confrontation with Uga V and by a last-second Georgia miracle that sent the game into overtime.

As Baker angled through the end zone and into Uga V's territory on the Georgia sidelines, he let loose of the football behind his back and began to showboat. Baker could've avoided Uga, who tried to get out of his way, but instead he came right at the six-year-old mascot. When it appeared they would collide, Uga went airborne, aiming for Baker's . . . *midsection,* to put it diplomatically. He might have made contact, but Baker put on the brakes and Charles Seiler pulled back on the leash—sparing Uga an unnecessary roughness penalty and Baker a trip to the hospital.

"Uga acted on instinct," says Sonny. "It wasn't that he wanted to *bite* Baker so much as *catch* him. He viewed him as a trespasser—and seeing him in our end zone scoring the game's first touchdown, Uga was right!"

As Baker backpedalled away from Uga, it appeared to some Georgia fans that he extended his index fingers as if firing two pistols at Uga—and all of this was captured live by the network camera crew. Georgia fans roared, and the CBS announcers made the most of it.

"Look where the ball's thrown—right to the corner and right at Uga," said color commentator Mike Mayock as the play was shown again on instant replay. "Now watch Baker . . . he almost gets bit by Uga . . . he says, 'Get away from me, man . . . it's tough enough to score without Uga biting me!'"

CBS went to a commercial break, then ran the tape again

[THEY SAID IT]

"ONE OF OUR FONDEST MEMORIES occurred during the last Georgia vs. Mississippi State game in Starkville [1996]. As the two handlers brought the two school mascots together, the MSU bulldog was so traumatized by Uga V that the handler actually had to carry the MSU bulldog off the field."

—E. Thomas Starcher II

Uga V

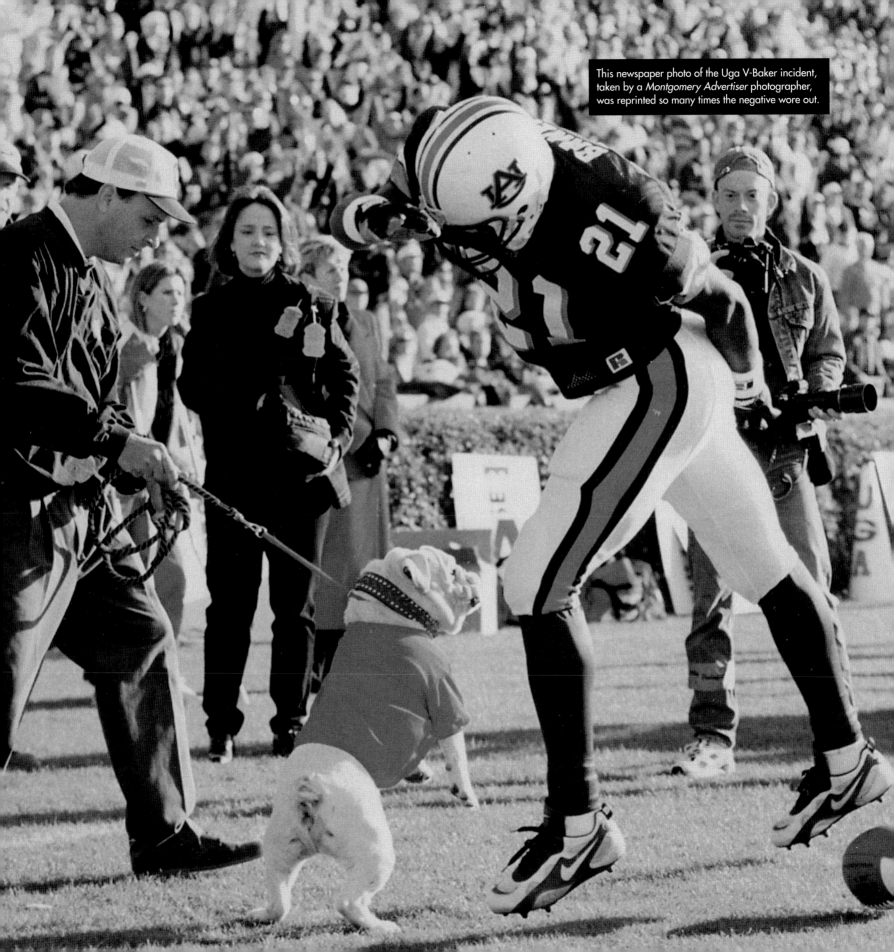

This newspaper photo of the Uga V-Baker incident, taken by a *Montgomery Advertiser* photographer, was reprinted so many times the negative wore out.

from a different camera angle as Mayock and play-by-play man Sean McDonough went on and on about Uga.

"The Georgia defense might want to consider dressing Uga!" said McDonough. "He went right after Robert Baker after the touchdown. We talked about the fierce rivalry . . . Uga has his game face on early!"

"Uga was a little more feisty than the Georgia defense in that first series, I'll tell you," said Mayock. "It's one of the classiest mascots in all of college football!"

When Corey Allen dropped a key pass in the fourth quarter, the TV camera showed Uga woof-woof-woofing encouragement from the sidelines. "Is he the best mascot you've ever seen, or what!" said Mayock. As Georgia snapped the ball on a crucial third-down play, McDonough said, "If they gave the ball to Uga, I think he'd get the 2 yards . . . instead they give it to [Robert] Edwards and it doesn't appear that he did."

Uga V's aggressiveness seemed to spark the Georgia team, which came from behind to tie the game 31-31 on a desperation 30-yard touchdown pass from quarterback Mike Bobo to Allen, who caught the ball at the goal line and fell into the end zone as time expired. Operating under the alternating possession rule, Georgia and Auburn swapped score after score until the Georgia defense held and the Dogs won a 56-49 thriller in quadruple overtime.

The rights to the Uga-Baker tape were purchased by ESPN, which showed it on *SportsCenter* and later dubbed it their "Play of the Year."

Video cameras weren't the only ones rolling at Auburn. A photographer from the *Montgomery Advertiser* also captured the Uga-Baker confrontation and the image became an instant collector's item after it was published in the Sunday edition of the paper.

The Uga-Baker photo was carried by news services all over the country and the *Montgomery Advertiser* received 1,000 reprint requests during the first three weeks following the game—and not just from Georgia fans. Crimson Tide loyalists also wanted the shot of Uga V challenging their in-state rival. To handle the

[THEY SAID IT]

"IF YOU CAN'T appreciate the swaggering gait and Churchillian physiognomy of Uga V, you must be a cat lover."

—*Sports Illustrated* in naming him the nation's No. 1 mascot

crush, the paper established an independent ordering system solely for the Uga-Baker photo.

"It felt like we were in the full-time Uga business," executive editor Paula Moore told the *Savannah Morning News.*

"The response was amazing," said assistant city editor Ken Roberts. "I can't think of anything else that would remotely rival that interest. Second place would be about fifteen or twenty requests."

The demand continued and a week before the '98 Georgia-Auburn game the *Advertiser* contacted UGA sports information director Claude Felton and told him to inform future callers that no more reprints could be made because the Uga-Baker negative had literally worn out.

Signature moment No. 2: *SI* cover dog

In April 1997, just four months after Uga V's run-in with Robert Baker made national news, a group of *Sports Illustrated* editors was burning the midnight oil on the eighteenth floor of the Time-Life Building in midtown Manhattan. For months, *SI* senior editor Craig Neff, design director Steve Hoffman, and photography director Steve Fine had been putting together a special college sports issue ["America's Top 50 Jock Schools," *SI*, April 28, 1997] that would give readers an insider's view of the nation's athletic powerhouses, with mini features on everything from famous alums to which schools have the best facilities, coaching shows, even must-visit sports bars. The hard work was mostly done and the issue was coming together nicely, though the most important step still remained, as Craig Neff explains:

"We had two candidates for the cover—Uga V or a posed UCLA-is-No. 1 shot featuring some Bruin football players and '96 Olympic gymnastics hero Kerri Strug, who was a student at UCLA. The initial plan was to go with UCLA, but when we dummied up that cover it just didn't capture the spirit of the issue. Uga did. Wearing that Georgia sweater, Uga had a classic, old-school, college-sports look. He brought a smile to the face of every *SI* editor who saw the photo."

Uga V

Including the man in charge, *SI*'s managing editor Bill Colson, who felt something was missing when Steve Hoffman showed him the mockup of the UCLA cover. "Let's try Uga," said Colson, who was beaming an hour later when he walked into Neff's office holding a printout of the new cover with Uga V's massive head extending almost to the top of the page, obscuring a significant portion of the familiar *Sports Illustrated* cover logo.

"Bill likes dogs," says Neff, "and he was rightly pleased with how good—and how different—this bulldog looked."

The cover shot was one of many images that Atlanta freelance photographer Greg Foster had taken of Uga V during a visit to Savannah several weeks earlier.

"I asked Greg at the time if he'd ever had a photo make the cover of *SI*. He said he hadn't but he'd sure like to," Sonny recalls. "'Work hard on Uga,' I told him, 'and maybe you'll get your wish.'"

Weeks went by and the Seilers forgot all about the jock-schools story and the photos Foster had taken of Uga.

"On the day the *SI* cover hit the news-stands, I was working at my office when the phone rang," Sonny recalls. "It was my friend and former colleague on UGA's alumni association board, Condace Pressley, from WSB Radio in Atlanta. She said, 'Have you seen *Sports Illustrated?* We are all very proud of Uga.' She went on to tell me that Uga was pictured alone on the cover of the magazine. . . . I was so excited that I can't remember any more of our conversation!"

Uga V's striking cover relegated the photo of gold medalist Strug and UCLA to the contents page, and *SI* paid further tribute to him in a "Best Mascot" box (right) with text that was brief and to the point:

"If you can't appreciate the swaggering gait and Churchillian physiognomy of Uga V, the Bulldog's bulldog, you must be a cat lover."

And speaking of cats, Uga V earned his best-mascot distinction at the expense of the King of Beasts: Leo, the University of North Alabama lion, finished second.

SI's definition of a jock school—any college or university in which sports are central to campus life . . . a place where sports-minded students can flourish . . . an institution that puts a premium on enjoying the "tailgating, Yale-baiting, cheerleading, beerbleeding sports scene"—certainly fit the University of Georgia. Except for that "Yale-baiting" part, seeing as how UGA's first two presidents were Yale grads. Georgia ranked No. 21 on *SI*'s list of the nation's athletic powerhouses, and its new forty million dollar fitness facility, the Ramsey Student Center for Physical Activities, ranked No. 1 among on-campus recreation centers.

UGA president Charles Knapp took it upon himself to write a congratulatory letter to Uga V. "This is a singular day for the university," Knapp wrote. "It is proof once again that you are the most well-known mascot in the United States, if not the world! Please

Uga V

"Uga had a classic, old-school, college-sports look," says *Sports Illustrated* senior editor Craig Neff, who was in charge of the special jock schools section of the April 28, 1997 issue. "He brought a smile to the face of every *SI* editor who saw the photo."

BEST MASCOT *Georgia.* If you can't appreciate the swaggering gait and Churchillian physiognomy of UGA V, the Bulldogs' bulldog, you must be a cat lover.

SECOND-BEST MASCOT *North Alabama.* O.K., so you're a cat lover. You'd purr for Leo II, a nine-year-old male lion whose outdoor caged compound is located only steps from the student union. He's considerably better behaved than his predecessor, the original Leo, who during a 1974 photo shoot nipped Miss Alabama on the posterior (or, as she put it, "punctuated" her visit).

MOST INDEFATIGABLE COSTUMED MASCOT *St. Joseph's.* The Hawk is required to flap his wings ceaselessly from the moment the St. Joe's basketball team takes the floor until the game ends.

know that I count this occasion among the very best of the highlights of my years as president."

It wasn't the swimsuit issue, but Georgians bought out *SI*'s Uga V cover almost as quickly. Only one other school mascot—Yale's Handsome Dan, who is also an English bulldog—has ever been featured on the cover of the nation's most revered sports magazine.

"Uga V isn't the first UGA mascot to appear in *SI*, but he is the first to command the cover," says Sonny, who told the media he purposely hadn't shown the issue to Uga. "His head will get so big, he won't be able to fit into his sweater."

Uga V

Athletic director Vince Dooley awarded Uga V a special medallion honoring him as "The Nation's No. 1 Mascot."

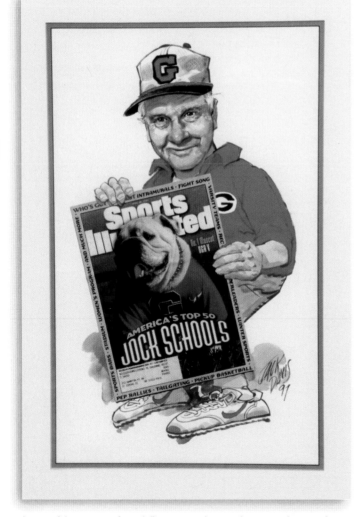

In honor of the *SI* cover, famed illustrator and UGA alumnus Jack Davis drew something for the wall of Sonny's den.

Sports Illustrated's definition of a jock school included one of Uga's favorite pastimes—tailgating! It's clear where these big and little cheerleaders' sentiments lie.

Uga V

In recognition of his *Sports Illustrated* cover and his participation in Savannah's annual St. Patrick's Day parade, Uga V received an honorary Doctor of Irish Literature degree from Armstrong Atlantic State University.

First *SI*, then National Public Radio

On April 30, 1997, shortly after Uga V's *Sports Illustrated* cover hit the newsstands, Sonny was interviewed by National Public Radio's Bob Edwards, host of "Morning Edition." The following is an excerpt from that interview:

Edwards: He's got a flat nose, a hairy face, and doggy breath, but a major magazine has voted him the best in his profession. His name is Uga, as in U-g-a. He's a bulldog, the official mascot for the University of Georgia, and he's on the cover of *Sports Illustrated* as the nation's best college mascot. Uga's owner is Sonny Seiler, a Savannah lawyer best known as one of the defense attorneys in the murder trial featured in John Berendt's book, *Midnight in the Garden of Good and Evil.* Seiler has owned and trained the Georgia mascot since 1956. The dogs change, but the name stays the same. Seiler says this Uga is the first to make the cover of *Sports Illustrated.*

Seiler: All of the Ugas have been in *Sports Illustrated* at one time or another, but usually in connection with stories on our football team or bowl games or things like that. So, to finally crack and get on the cover was a compliment to the University of Georgia and our fine athletic program—and especially Uga.

Edwards: Is Uga a he or a she?

Seiler: Oh, very much a he.

Edwards: Have all the Ugas been he's?

Seiler: They have. And although there is nothing that says that the gender can't change, they are a little more durable and calmer than a female.

Edwards: What breed is Uga exactly?

Seiler: English bulldog.

Edwards: English bull, yeah. And what qualities does Uga have that make him such a good mascot?

Seiler: Just his pleasant disposition, which is inherent with that breed. They get along fine with people. Crowd noise doesn't bother them. Heat is really their biggest enemy down here.

Edwards: But do you want a mascot with a pleasing disposition? I mean we're talking football here. I mean . . .

Seiler: Well, we want one because he travels with the team and he's around people all the time. The breed is not an aggressive breed, but he's ferocious looking. Let me put it this way to you— if I put him in the car and don't lock him up, there are not many people gonna steal him.

(Laughter)

Edwards: Have you ever thought of turning Uga loose on an Alabama halfback?

Seiler: Nah, he wouldn't go after him. Now, he jumped at an Auburn player, but only because the Auburn player ran out of the end zone and came over and startled him. But if he'd gotten him, he would've known it!

#1 mascot in the country
UGA V

University of Georgia
1997-98 STUDENT • FACULTY • STAFF DIRECTORY

Once you've made the cover of *SI*, everybody wants a piece of you.

Uga V

Uga V

If Uga ever gets sick, professional wrestler [Bill] Goldberg—a football standout at Georgia—would make a very convincing substitute.

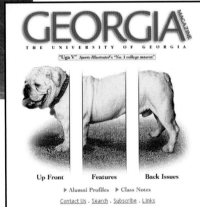

To get to *Georgia Magazine*'s online edition, (www.uga.edu/gm), readers have to go through Uga V.

Uga V

Midnight in the Garden of Good and Evil (The Movie) was directed by Clint Eastwood, who cast both Sonny and Uga V in the film version of John Berendt's bestseller.

Signature moment No. 3:
Uga goes Hollywood . . . and so does Sonny!

Earlier in the week, before the *SI* cover had hit the newsstands, the phone rang in Sonny's law office. His secretary answered.

"Mr. Eastwood calling for Sonny Seiler."

Clint Eastwood (A.K.A. Dirty Harry, Pale Rider, Man With No Name) was calling to offer Uga V the part of his father, Uga IV, in the film version of John Berendt's record-breaking bestseller, *Midnight in the Garden of Good and Evil,* which Eastwood was set to direct. Berendt's tale of death and decadence in Savannah spent more weeks on *The New York Times* Best Seller list than any hardback in history—fiction or nonfiction—surpassing *The Robe* and *The Power of Positive Thinking.* In preparation for shooting the film version, Eastwood had been quietly slipping in and out of Savannah to scout locations.

Atlanta has *Gone With the Wind,* and now Savannah has *Midnight in the Garden of Good and Evil*—which literally reinvented the Savannah tourist industry, giving the city a dark, sexy, international identity that green beer and St. Patty's Day never could. Berendt's bestseller produced a forty-six percent spike in Savannah's tourist trade and a bookstore-museum on Calhoun Square filled with every kind of *Midnight* paraphernalia imaginable, from souvenir maps to commemorative cookie tins. As Eastwood told *USA Today:*

"When you go down there, everybody has The Book on sale. In most towns, they're talking about the Bible, but not here. The Book is sold in drugstores and candy stores and baby stores—you name it."

Ginger Duncan, owner of the Antique Bookstore, originally bought fifty copies of *Midnight* just because she knew and liked Berendt. A year later, the proceeds from *Midnight* sales alone enabled her to buy a new Buick.

"Initially, there was great speculation as to what role Clint would play in the movie," says Sonny, who can look out his office window at Bouhan, Williams & Levy and see tour guides stopping their trolleys in front of 447 Bull Street to tell passengers that he is the attorney who got Jim Williams acquitted in the *Midnight* murder trial. "And then came the announcement that Clint would direct the movie with a screenplay by John Lee Hancock, who happens to be a lawyer himself."

Sonny conferred frequently with Hancock on the script, and his office, located in the Armstrong House mansion that his law firm

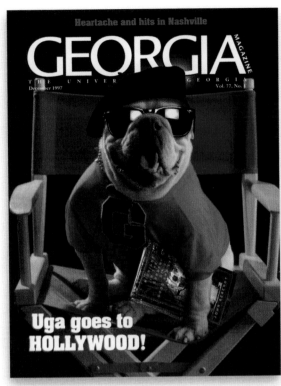

Heartache and hits in Nashville

GEORGIA

December 1997   Vol. 77, No.

Uga goes to HOLLYWOOD!

Uga V on the cover of the UGA alumni magazine.

purchased from antiques dealer Jim Williams, was chosen for several scenes. As the weeks went by, the cast began to take shape. Kevin Spacey was chosen to play Williams, John Cusack would play Berendt (known as John Kelso in the film), English actor Jude Law would play Williams' lover Danny Hansford (known as Billy Hanson in the film), and Sonny would be played by noted Australian actor Jack Thompson, whom American audiences remember from "Breaker Morant."

But who would play Uga IV, who made it into Berendt's book because of his never-ending devotion—and Sonny's—to the University of Georgia?

On a chilly Saturday morning in mid-April, Eastwood flew to Savannah to visit Williams' mansion and to try to convince his sister, Dorothy Kingery, to let him film scenes there. He also wanted to size up Uga V's acting ability.

"Cecelia brought Uga V to my office that Saturday morning, and when Clint walked in he took an immediate liking to the dog," says Sonny. "You should have seen the two of them. Clint got down on the floor and was wrestling with Uga. Clint was rubbing his head when he said, 'Uga, I'm going to make you a celebrity.'"

At which point, the seldom-bashful Cecelia delivered a classic rejoinder:

"Mr. Eastwood, Uga is *already* a celebrity."

Having played a starring role in Jim Williams' real-world rollercoaster ride through the judicial system, Sonny hoped for an inconspicuous role in Eastwood's film—as a juror perhaps.

"I thought it would be a hoot to serve on the jury that finally acquits my client," says Sonny, who saved Williams' hide in murder trial #4 with a Hollywood-style revelation about a hidden clue on a hospital admission sheet.

Shortly before filming started in May 1997, Eastwood asked Sonny a leading question:

"Have you ever done any acting?"

"Whenever I go to court," Sonny shot back.

"Seriously," said Eastwood. "I'd like you to play the judge. You've got the looks, the voice, you're the right age, and you can advise me on courtroom stuff."

When a Hollywood legend, says, in effect, "Make my day by playing this part in my movie," what's a fella to do? So Sonny Seiler—diehard Georgia football fan, patriarch of the Uga mascots, past president of the State Bar of Georgia and the UGA Alumni Association—joined the Screen Actors Guild.

Uga V

To master Sonny's accent and bombastic courtroom style, lookalike Australian actor Jack Thompson (shown here with Sonny in Forsyth Park and filming a scene at Sonny's actual office desk) spent long hours listening to courtroom tapes of Sonny from the Williams trial.

"Sonny" Seiler is pictured here with Ed Sprouse, the newest associate of the Bouhan, Williams & Levy law firm. Ed received the Outstanding Senior Award in the most recent graduating class of the U. Ga. Law School. In the background is the former Armstrong Mansion, recently bought and adapted for offices by Seiler's firm.

November, 1971   5

As a young lawyer at the Savannah firm of Bouhan, Williams & Levy, Sonny (at right in this 1971 photo) never dreamed he would one day win a murder case that would land him a part in a movie directed by Clint Eastwood. Shown rehearsing a scene with Eastwood, Jack Thompson, and the director's other surprising casting decision—Lady Chablis as Lady Chablis —Sonny subsequently appeared in two other feature films: *The Gingerbread Man* and *The Legend of Bagger Vance.*

Uga V

Uga V did too. But apparently, the animal trainers for *Midnight* didn't have as much confidence in him as Eastwood did because they brought along a stand-in, a white male English bulldog named Beauregard.

"They brought Beauregard to my office in a cage, thinking he might be used in the event Uga V was not up to the task—but Big Beau never had a chance," says Sonny. "To begin with, he was grossly overweight and would've had trouble performing in Savannah's heat. But that's a moot point because Uga V's performance in the movie was letter-perfect."

Shortly after the opening credits, Jim Williams [Spacey] and John Kelso [Cusack] take Uga for a walk in nearby Forsyth Park, where a pretty girl rushes up and asks if they will take her picture with the Georgia mascot. Uga doesn't flinch when the girl puts her arms around him because she's played by the Seilers' middle daughter, Bess Seiler Thompson, who grew up with the mascots.

Shortly after the opening credits, Uga V is taken for a walk through Forsyth Park by Kevin Spacey and John Cusack. Between takes, Uga V relaxes with Cusack and Clint Eastwood's daughter, actress Alison Eastwood, who also appeared in the film.

"The next line is priceless," says Sonny. "Probably the best line in the whole movie."

Williams: Neither one of us will ever be as famous as that dog.

Kelso: Who's that dog?

Williams: Why, that's Uga, the University of Georgia mascot. He's better known than we'll ever be.

As would be the case with any motion picture, some of Sonny's and Uga's scenes ended up on the cutting-room floor—including an airport scene where the University of Georgia occupied center stage.

"John Kelso knows I'm totally University of Georgia-oriented—and a football nut," says Sonny, whose den is a shrine to Uga and Georgia athletics. "When he finds out I'm going to the Dogs' season opener on the eve of the Jim Williams trial, he can't believe it."

The scene was shot at a private airport in Savannah where crowds of Georgia fans have come out to give the Seilers a great sendoff to a fictional game against Notre Dame, which is being played in Athens. There's a Bulldog decal on the plane, a contingent of Georgia alums cheering wildly, and everyone is decked out in their best red-and-black football garb.

"People are waving UGA pennants in the background—and here comes Seiler, struttin' along with Uga on a leash," says Sonny, as giddy about the scene now as when he watched Eastwood shoot it. "And here's Kelso, begging me not to go because we're at a critical juncture in the Williams case, and he feels I'm coppin' out by leaving town."

When Sonny says, "I'm coppin' out," he's referring to his alter-ego, actor Jack Thompson, who listened to boxes of cassettes from the actual Williams trial in order to master Sonny's "Geechee" Savannah accent and bombastic courtroom style. The airport scene ends on a dramatic note as Thompson—who looks enough like Sonny to be his brother—boards the plane, then turns back to the crowd. He breaks into an animated, thumbs-up crouch, and then yells at the top of his lungs, "GO DOGS!!!"

Watching the scene unfold from his usual position next to camera No. 1, Eastwood had a big smile on his face—and a Georgia cap on his head.

"Between takes, we had to stand on the tarmac—and so did all those big stars with the sun beating down on them," says Sonny. "But the minute we took a break, the trainers would come dashing out to fan Uga. They even held an umbrella over him!"

Uga V

One of the scenes that didn't make the movie's final cut was shot at a private airport in Savannah, where crowds of Georgia fans gathered to give Sonny and Uga a big sendoff prior to a football game in Athens. Two of the extras were the Seilers' granddaughters (from left, Margaret Story and Sara Thompson), shown here with actor Jack Thompson.

Uga V

Sonny was surprised by two aspects of Eastwood's movie-making style: few auditions and no rehearsals.

"He knows who he wants to play the parts, and we were expected to show up ready to shoot," says Sonny. "I wanted to do a good job, so I memorized my lines. And, for the most part, I wasn't nervous in front of the camera. If I'd been asked to play a doctor, an astronaut, or an engineer, I would've been in trouble. A judge, I can handle. But I did think we'd rehearse the scenes . . . there were zero rehearsals."

Sonny recalls a critical courtroom scene where the Seiler character cross-examines a Savannah detective, asking him whether Danny Hansford's hands were bagged for powder burn tests. Williams claimed Hansford shot at him first, and that he fired back in self-defense. Forensic tests revealed no traces of gunpowder on Hansford's hands, but Sonny discovered that Hansford's hands weren't actually bagged until he arrived at the hospital, thus invalidating the powder burn tests and making Williams' explanation of the sequence of events plausible to the jury.

"When the actors showed up to shoot that complicated scene, they'd never even met, let alone rehearsed," says Sonny. "But you should have seen it unfold. Clint asked them if they were comfortable with their parts and if they had any questions. Then, in a quiet voice, he said, 'Camera No. 1 ready? Camera No. 2 ready? Okay . . . we're . . . rolling.'"

[THEY SAID IT]

"UGA V IS NO HOUSE PET. He's quite used to performing before 80,000 rabid Georgia fans every Saturday in the fall. His bloodlines show—he's an ultimate professional, camera-ready and walking and slobbering on command."

—*Midnight* screenwriter John Lee Hancock

The witness stand sequence that followed was so good that Eastwood shot it straight through in one take.

"I was paralyzed," says Sonny, who watched from the judge's bench. "These guys are going through this tough dialogue bang-bang-bang and acting up a storm . . . watching them, I lost track of whether I had any lines. Thank God, I didn't!"

Midnight in the Garden of Good and Evil premiered in Hollywood, as was to be expected, and also in Savannah, in deference to a city gone certifiably nuts over The Book. Not as in, "Have you *read* The Book" because, of course, everyone has. But rather, "Who do you know who's *in* The Book?"

Minus the leadership of the late Jim Williams, whose legendary parties were what attracted *Esquire* columnist Berendt to the city in the first place, Savannahians marked the movie premiere with Hollywood-style soirees of their own design. The city constructed reviewing stands, installed search lights, and rolled out a long red carpet to greet Kevin Spacey and his co-stars—Sonny and Uga V included—as they emerged from limousines and entered the Savannah Civic Center for the premiere of *Midnight*.

"It was an incredible night—for me, for Uga, and for Savannah," says Sonny. "Nonie Sutton made Uga a new tux for the big event, and as Charles led him into the civic center the

On-stage to help warm up the crowd at the "Midnight" premiere were (from left): Savannah congressman Jack Kingston, Sonny, actor Paul Hipp (who played Joe Odum), Charles Seiler, Jack Thompson, Kevin Spacey, and, of course, Uga V!

flash cameras were really popping. He got as much attention as any of the actors—Kevin Spacey included."

Onstage to help Spacey warm up the crowd were Jack Thompson, Savannah congressman Jack Kingston, Sonny—and the tuxedoed Uga V, who nearly upstaged the ultra-charming Spacey.

"The event was covered by all of the major news outlets and Uga found himself in *Sports Illustrated* again, modeling his tux on the red carpet," Sonny recalls. "After the movie, Uga V attended a gala reception with the rest of the cast. He passed on the champagne but did a helluva job on the finger sandwiches and cake. On the way home, he looked up at me in the limo, as if to say, 'That was fun, boss! When can we do it again?'"

Uga V

Sports Illustrated's "Show Dog" premiere story began: "He was short, about 50 pounds, with handsome, almost sinister features, white fur, a prodigious underbite, and eyes (and snout) as black as the tinted windows of the sleek limousine from which he had just emerged."

"If I'd been asked to play a doctor, an astronaut , or an engineer, I would've been in trouble," says Sonny of his film debut. "A judge I can handle."

There are few things Uga likes better than going for a boat ride with Sonny.

Uga's movie and TV credits

Uga V

Uga V's portrayal of his father, Uga IV, in Warner Brothers' *Midnight in the Garden of Good and Evil* was not the first time a member of the mascot line had appeared on the silver screen.

Uga III appeared in *Gator,* which starred Burt Reynolds and was also shot in Savannah. His scene was filmed at the old Oglethorpe Hotel on Wilmington Island, where Cecelia and Uga III are seen in the background coming up the walkway to the hotel. Cecelia made fifty dollars as an extra and Uga III got a free meal.

In 1983, Uga IV was selected to play an English bulldog named Winston in *Six Pack,* a television spin-off from the movie *Six Pack,* which starred Kenny Rogers. The TV version was produced by Gy Waldron Productions in association with Twentieth Century Fox Television.

Nowhere Productions, an independent film company based in Athens, has produced *Damn Good Dog!,* a video history of the Georgia mascots that features recent footage of Uga V and VI. Producer-director Erica McCarthy and her staff followed the Seilers and their dogs around, off and on, for two years and conducted numerous interviews with people who have known and been associated with the dogs over the years.

Turner Broadcasting System recently released a video feature, *A Day in the Life of the Georgia Mascot,* Turner South featured Uga VI in an episode of *Liars & Legends,* that won an Emmy Award, and Cineflix, Inc. of Montreal, Quebec, featured Uga VI in its TV series, *Dogs with Jobs.*

It's a tossup as to who's more popular in Athens—Uga or Santa.

Uga V goes out in style on national TV . . . where else?

With Uga V wearing the spiked collar, the mascot line made a quantum leap to a whole new level of celebrity. In nine seasons as the symbol of Georgia athletics, Uga V made more high-level public appearances than all of his predecessors combined.

Unfortunately, all that gallivanting around took its toll on Uga V, who was diagnosed with arthritis in his back legs in 1999. As any human being who suffers from arthritis will tell you, even low-impact activities such as walking can be difficult—and so it was for Uga V, who no longer took delight in racing around the Seilers' yard or roughhousing with the family.

"A Georgia Bulldog mascot needs to be virile, healthy, and active," says Sonny. "He must

THE REAL STAR OF THE OUTBACK BOWL

Paws & effect

As the Uga dynasty stretched into its fifth decade this season, Uga V raised the bar of popularity, becoming a dog as heroic as Rin Tin Tin and as lovable as Lassie.

By Timothy Guidera
Savannah Morning News

Like most celebrities, he's different at home, more relaxed, less aware of his status. Away from his fame, he can be unassuming, easily pleased and guilty of the commonest of comforts.

A familiar chair.

A faithful routine of dining and napping.

A favorite chew toy covered with his own slobber and teeth marks.

OK, so maybe Uga V is not the typical celebrity. But he is, in every sense, a major star.

UGA IV's Magillicuddy II, as he is registered, has served as the mascot for the University of Georgia's sports teams for eight years, but only recently has Uga V become a crossover star of unquestioned appeal. He is fifth in a line of purebred English screwtail bulldogs owned by Savannahians Sonny and Cecelia Seiler and provided by them as an ambassador to their alma mater in one of the university's richest and oldest traditions. But he has become first in broad recognition.

• • •

"This one seems to enjoy it more than the others did," Cecelia Seiler, Uga's primary care-giver at home, says of the current mascot. "He likes the attention more. He just loves being around people and being a part of everything. He is just a nice dog."

As the only male pup in the final litter fathered by his predecessor, perhaps notoriety was Uga V's birthright. But unbridled stardom has been this dog's unique bend on the Uga legend that this season entered its fifth decade.

See **UGA**, Page **3A**

Photos by Scott Bryant/Savannah Morning News

A few of the amenities afforded such a special dawg

Uga's special silver bowl is inscribed with the words "Let the Big Dog Eat" on one side and Uga V on the other.

Uga's custom-made jersey is complete with a Nike swoosh. The wardrobe is made special for each dog: No hand-me-downs here.

Uga's red, spiked collar has a personalized tag. Each dog, after its time here is done, is buried with its own collar.

This travel bag contains all of Uga's game gear and when it is brought out, Uga knows it's time to go to Athens for a game.

This bulldog angel sits atop the Seilers' Christmas tree. It is one of the homemade items that pay tribute to the famous dogs.

Uga V served as grand marshal of UGA's 1998 Homecoming parade. It was his last public appearance.

On January 1, 1998, with Georgia kicking off New Year's Day's non-stop college football action at the Outback Bowl in Tampa, Savannahians opened their morning paper to a front-page feature on Uga V, who was deemed "as heroic as Rin Tin Tin and as lovable as Lassie" by the *Savannah Morning News*.

portray the qualities of dignity, courage, and strength. He has to be able to travel well and he must be durable. Uga V had enjoyed a great run, but he needed to step aside and let his son, Uga VI, take over."

After consulting with Coach Dooley and Uga V's doctors at the UGA vet school, the Seilers decided that the changing of the collar ceremony would take place sometime during the early part of the '99 season. They also decided to announce his retirement before Picture Day in August so his devoted fans would have a last opportunity to get a photo taken with him before he retired.

"Although it was hard for him to stand," says Sonny, "Uga posed with adoring fans for more than two hours before we had to close the line so he could rest."

Uga V started the '99 season, which began with a 38-7 victory over Utah State in Athens, then retired prior to the second home

Saturday, October 17, 1998

GAMEDAY

Where no dog has gone before

Uga V breaking new ground again

By Shane Hannon
Staff Writer

Uga V continues to go where no dog — or mascot — has gone before.

First, the Bulldog was featured on the cover of Sports Illustrated in the spring of 1997 as the No. 1 mascot in the country, then later that year made his film debut in Clint Eastwood's Midnight in the Garden of Good and Evil.

And the pioneer for mascots continues to set the standard in 1998. Uga's latest move into the

sure the dog wasn't inhibited in anyway," said the younger Seiler. "Actually, Uga doesn't even notice it all."

Here's how Uga-cam works: the video signal is sent from the "lipstick" camera (meaning it's about the size of a lipstick) through a wire which runs up Uga's leash into the fanny pack worn by Seiler. A cable then runs from the fanny pack to someone holding a microwave transmitter (looks like a pole with a flat antennae). The microwaves carrying the signal is the sent from the antennae through the air to McCarthy in the press box, where she can see the image and program it into the stadium screen.

"I think the fans like it,"

Jeff Blake/Photo staff
Uga V and his collar-mounted camera keep an eye on things.

Uga V

The Uga Cam relays images from a miniature video camera mounted on Uga's back to the giant matrix scoreboard at Sanford Stadium. It's a real crowd favorite, but it did get Uga V into a bit of trouble when he accidentally pointed the camera under a cheerleader's skirt.

game against South Carolina on September 11. With ESPN2 cameras there to record the pregame ceremony, Uga V was led to the 50-yard line just prior to kickoff. Uga VI was there too, along with members of the Seiler family. The crowd roared when a replay of Uga V's encounter with Auburn's Robert Baker was shown on the giant matrix screen.

"As the dogs were led from the field," says Sonny, "Uga V displayed a much livelier gait. He positively swaggered to the sidelines as the crowd let loose with 'Damn Good Dog!!! . . . Damn Good Dog!!! . . . Damn Good Dog!'"

ESPN replayed the pre-game ceremonies during the telecast of the game, which ended with the Bulldogs on top 24-9. As Coach Dooley said, "It was quite a day."

Uga V's last lap as mascot created a media frenzy.

Uga V dies at home from congestive heart failure

Just two months after Uga V retired, he began to slip. It was hard for him to get up, he wasn't interested in eating, and he didn't want to walk. Cecelia dropped him off at the local vet, who examined him and found nothing wrong that the Seilers didn't already know about. At his retirement two months earlier, Uga V was a healthy dog with the exception of the arthritis.

"Uga's vet, Dr. Stanley Lester, called me and said Uga V had rallied," says Cecelia. "He said that when they took him outside he walked around and seemed to be doing all right."

Cecelia brought Uga V home, but on that same day, November 22, 1999, he succumbed to congestive heart failure at around five o'clock in the afternoon.

"When these dogs go," says Sonny, "they go fast."

Sonny called Coach Dooley and told him that Uga had died. The next day, Charles and Sonny took him to Athens in his traveling kennel for burial with his forefathers in Sanford Stadium.

Coach Jim Donnan told the press that Uga V's death was "a loss to our football program and the university. He served my teams well for three years and represented all the things we want in a mascot and team—strength, courage, dignity, and pride."

The entire Donnan family loved Uga. In fact, when they arrived in Athens, they, too, had an English bulldog. His name was Reggie.

"I think most will agree that Uga V was perhaps the most popular of all the mascots, primarily due to his national and international notoriety," said Dooley. "He set a great standard and left a great legacy for his son, Uga VI, to lead all of us into the 21st century."

Uga V

When ESPN's college football "Game Day" crew (from left, Chris Fowler, Lee Corso, and Kirk Herbstreit) came to Athens prior to the Dogs' 1998 game against Tennessee, they asked Uga V to make an appearance on their show.

The difference in size was obvious as Uga V (left) and Uga VI mimic the same pose that Uga I and Uga II struck at their changing-of-the-collar ceremony more than three decades earlier (see p. 25).

Vince Dooley decided that Uga V's funeral should be open to the public. Offering his condolences to Sonny was retired tennis coach and sports information director Dan Magill, who helped him get the mascot line started back in 1956.

Uga V

Uga V is buried at Sanford Stadium

All of the other mascot burials had been private affairs. But due to Uga V's popularity and fame, the athletic department decided to publicly announce plans for his interment. The mascot vaults at the southwest corner of Sanford Stadium had been beautifully renovated following the 1996 Olympics. An impressive wall of Georgia red marble now houses the vaults of the deceased dogs, whose achievements are engraved on bronze memorial tablets. Standing guard over the graves is the striking life-size bronze statue of Uga by sculptor Wyndell Taylor.

Uga V's vault was open and prepared when the Seilers arrived.

"It's so sad to pull into our usual game-day parking place under the bridge—but for a much different reason," says Sonny, who was heartened to see hundreds of students lining the bridge above as Uga V's coffin was rolled into the stadium in his kennel. The attendees included athletic officials, alumni personnel, and many friends. President Michael Adams was on a trip but his wife, Mary, and members of the president's staff were in attendance. Uga V's official namesake, Dan Magill, was there, too.

Coach Dooley began the ceremony by observing that Uga V never shunned publicity, thus explaining why the athletic department decided to set aside the custom of private mascot burials. He recounted Uga V's many accomplishments and publicly thanked the Seilers for making the dogs such an integral part of the University of Georgia. He paid a special tribute to Cecelia Seiler, who did not make the trip. Representing the family were Sonny and Charles and Sara Seiler Story, who placed a wreath over the vault that had been presented to the Seilers by director of alumni relations Dave Muia on behalf of all UGA alumni.

Following Dooley's remarks, Reverand Claude McBride, long-time chaplain for UGA athletic teams and a classmate of Cecelia's at Columbus High School, delivered a beautiful eulogy. He offered a prayer, which began:

"All creatures great and small, the Lord God made them all."

McBride praised Uga V for the spirit and pride that he had instilled in all Georgia Bulldogs, concluding his eulogy by saying, "As Uga was so aptly praised by our students, thank you, Father, for a Damn Good Dog."

For Sonny and Charles, the ride back to Savannah was quiet and lonely; a beloved passenger and long-time companion had been left behind. Fran Hohenstein, a longtime friend of the Seiler family, sent a touching memorial to Uga V.

The Rainbow Bridge

Just this side of heaven is a place called Rainbow Bridge.
When an animal dies that has been especially close to
    someone here, that pet goes to Rainbow Bridge.
There are meadows and hills for all of our special friends
    so they can run and play together.
There is plenty of food, water, and sunshine, and our friends
    are warm and comfortable.

All the animals who had been ill and old are restored to
    health and vigor; those who were hurt or maimed are made
    whole and strong again, just as we remember them in our
    dreams of days gone by.
The animals are happy and content, except for one small thing:
    they each miss someone very special to them who had to be
    left behind.
They all run and play together, but the day comes when one
    suddenly stops and looks into the distance.
His bright eyes are intent, his eager body quivers.
Suddenly, he begins to run from the group, flying over the green
    grass, his legs carrying him faster and faster.

You have been spotted, and when you and your special friend
    finally meet, you cling together in joyous reunion, never to be
    parted again.
The happy kisses rain upon your face, your hands again caress
    the beloved head, and you look once more into the trusting
    eyes of your pet, so long gone from your life but never absent
    from your heart.

Then you cross the Rainbow Bridge together.

—Author unknown

On the Sunday after Uga V died, the *Atlanta Journal-Constitution* ran a letter to the editor at the bottom of its main editorial page. It was written by retired Atlanta anesthesiologist Conrad Freeman and it spoke volumes about the extent of Uga V's popularity:

"No, I did not attend the University of Georgia, but I sure did love that old bulldog, Uga V. There was just something about him that people could relate to. I guess it was his big ol' sloppy love!"

Uga V

UGA V
GEORGIA MASCOT
1990-1999
FIRST HONORARY MEMBER
UGA
NATIONAL ALUMNI
ASSOCIATION
MOVIE STAR
6 BOWL TEAMS
8 NATIONAL CHAMPIONSHIP
TEAMS
"NATION'S NUMBER 1
COLLEGE MASCOT"
SPORTS ILLUSTRATED, 1997
"DEFENDER OF HIS TURF"

Uga VI
1999–

Born
July 22, 1998

AKC registered name
Uga V's Whatchagot Loran?

Dates of service
September 11, 1999
to –

Football record
23-12 (1999–2001)

Bowl record
2-1

beat Purdue 28-25
in '00 Outback Bowl

beat Virginia 37-14
in '00 Oahu Bowl

lost to Boston College 20-16
in '01 Music City Bowl

Uga VI

A Big Dog for a Big Job

Uga IV and Uga V were still frisky little pups when they were called upon to serve as mascot. Special cut-down jerseys had to be made for their debuts, and the spiked collar was something their adolescent bodies had to grow into. But when Uga VI was introduced to the Sanford Stadium crowd on September 11, 1999, it was obvious that, in terms of size, this new-generation mascot stood head and shoulders above his famous father.

"It had been twenty-seven years since a full-grown dog had taken over the job," says Sonny, "and photographers and fans couldn't get over how much bigger Uga VI was compared to Uga V. You could tell the difference from the upper deck!"

Uga VI outweighed Uga V by 11 pounds, with a special jersey of his own from Claudia

When Uga VI took over as mascot on September 11, 1999, it had been twenty-seven years since a full-grown dog had donned the spiked collar. The difference in size between Uga VI and his famous father was evident to all who watched the changing-of-the-collar ceremony.

Warthen's big-and-tall shop. Seeing father and son together was like looking at a 270-pound lineman from the 1990s standing next to one of today's 330-pound behemoths.

"When we tried one of Uga V's jerseys on Uga VI," says Cecelia, "he looked like a sausage!"

The pregame changing-of-the-collar ceremony created a media frenzy with photographers jockeying for position as though they were covering a heavyweight title fight. UGA president Michael Adams waded through the phalanx of lenses and knelt at Uga V's side. He removed the spiked collar from the most famous dog in America and fastened it around the considerably broader neck of his impatient son.

"When we did the collar exchange," Adams would say later, "everybody had tears in their eyes—Sonny, Cecelia, Vince, and me."

Believe it or not, there are, in fact, two dogs in the midst of all those cameras.

Uga VI

Charles Seiler leads Uga VI onto the Sanford Stadium turf for the first time.

UGA president Michael Adams makes it official by fastening the spiked collar around Uga VI's neck.

"It's always the same . . . I've seen all six," said Dooley, who reminded the press that his career parallels the mascots'. Uga I was the mascot when he was named head coach at Georgia in 1964. And Dooley remembers seeing Uga I in action even before that, when he was a young assistant coach at Auburn watching from the Sanford Stadium press box as Uga I delighted the crowd by chewing up a toy War Eagle.

Georgia fans had begun applauding as both dogs made their way to the changing-of-the-collar ceremony, and their admiration for the mascots was obvious from conversations they had with *Athens Daily News* writer Ben Deck.

"It gave me chills!" said Ashley Prather, speaking for everyone in the student section.

Traditionally, a female cheerleader leads the mascot onto the field ahead of the players prior to kickoff. But with the outsized Uga VI taking the field for the first time, a change seemed to be in order.

"They said a girl couldn't handle him," said female cheerleading captain Shannon Massey.

Male cheerleading captain Clay Owensby was asked to handle Uga VI's leash during the pre-kickoff run-on. "I'm just going to hold on tight!" said

Traditionally, a female cheerleader leads the mascot onto the field ahead of the players prior to kickoff. But Uga VI is so big, the guys were told to man the leash.

Uga VI ran into old friend J.T. Ricketson at the 2000 Outback Bowl in Tampa. A mild-mannered Fort Valley druggist during the week, J.T. turns into "Super Dawg" on football Saturdays.

Owensby, sounding like he had the Colorado buffalo or Bevo, the Texas longhorn, in tow.

Photographers had surrounded both dogs when they came onto the field, and now—as Uga V retreated to the sidelines for the final time—they trained their lenses on Uga VI as he took up residence in an air-conditioned doghouse that now belonged to him. Up in the stands, even South Carolina fans were impressed.

"Nice-looking dog," said Paul Pickens. "You have a good thing going. Everyone knows about Uga."

Even the Gamecock cheerleaders got caught up in the moment.

"I thought it was really cute," said Jennifer Commella. "It was *awesome!*" said Shawn Dawkins.

Two quick bowl victories . . . and a no show at the luau

Jim Donnan was in his fourth year as head football coach at Georgia when Uga VI donned the spiked collar in 1999, and it was a good year for a mascot to debut. The Bulldogs finished the regular season 7-4 and earned a return trip to the Outback Bowl in Tampa, Florida, where two years earlier they had trounced Wisconsin 33-6. The Outback traditionally kicks off twelve hours of New Year's Day college football action, and the 11 A.M. kickoff was especially brutal for Georgia fans because this wasn't just any New Year's morning. It was Millennium Morning, January 1, 2000, and many of the red-and-black loyalists en route to the stadium for the Dogs' Outback Bowl meeting with Purdue were still bleary-eyed from celebrating Millennium Madness the night before.

The Seilers had spent the evening with Tampa residents Doug and Jean Ann Cone, who treated Sonny, Cecelia, Swann, Charles, and his wife Wendy (and later in the evening, Uga VI) to a stone crab-and-steak dinner at Malio's Restaurant. Jean Ann had invited a crowd of friends and relatives, including Tom McEwen, long-time sportswriter for the *Tampa Tribune*. Uga VI was a welcome guest and his red jersey attracted a steady stream of picture requests from Bulldog fans. Restaurant owner Malio Iavarone even got into the act.

"We didn't tell Uga about the stone crab claws," says Sonny, "but he did enjoy some leftover steak in a doggie bag later in the evening. When we picked up the paper the next day, Tom McEwen had included our party—and Uga VI—in his column."

The Georgia players had a New Year's Eve curfew but still had trouble getting on track the next morning, as Purdue rode the arm of its All-America quarterback Drew Brees to a 25-0 second-quarter lead. But with Uga VI barking encouragement from the sidelines, Georgia quarterback Quincy Carter staged some heroics of his own, rallying the Bulldogs to a 28-25 overtime victory before 54,000 fans and a national TV audience.

The game-winning field goal was kicked by Hap Hines, son of Justice Harris Hines of the Georgia Supreme Court. Hap got to be such a fan of Uga that his family gave him a direct descendant of the Georgia mascot as a graduation present.

Georgia posted another 7-4 regular season in 2000, and accepted a bid to play frequent bowl opponent Virginia in the Oahu Bowl in Honolulu. The trip to an exotic locale like Hawaii was a treat for the Georgia players, coaches, and fans—but Uga VI had to watch the game on TV in Savannah.

"We were all excited when Georgia accepted the invitation to go to Honolulu, and Uga VI already had his mouth set for roast pig at a Hawaiian luau," says Sonny. "But then we received a distressing telephone call from Georgia assistant athletic director Charlie Whittemore, who advised us that if Uga made the trip he could not attend the game because animals brought to Hawaii must be quarantined for two weeks. It was such a bummer that we all stayed home!"

Fortunately, Quincy Carter turned in another standout postseason performance and Georgia won its fourth consecutive bowl game 37-14.

The 2001 team posted an 8-3 regular season record under new coach Mark Richt and expected to be invited back to Tampa for a third Outback Bowl appearance in five years. But when LSU upset Tennessee in the SEC Championship game, Georgia ended up playing Boston College in the Music City Bowl in Nashville. Time ran out as the Dogs lost to the men from Beantown 20-16.

Uga VI

(above) Uga's first photo request often occurs as soon as he walks out of his suite at the Georgia Center. (below) Wendy Seiler takes Uga VI for his morning walk.

Uga VI

When the University of Georgia opened a posh new alumni club on the second floor of the Atlanta Financial Center in Buckhead, the Seilers got dressed up— Uga VI included. A portrait of Uga V was presented to the club on the occasion of Sonny completing his term as the first president of UGA's National Alumni Association. A jersey worn by Uga II is also on display.

A mascot for all seasons

Most people associate the mascot with Georgia football, but when it comes to other UGA athletic teams Uga is an equal opportunity supporter. Media guide photos, promotional posters, posing with players, appearing at games and matches—you name it and Uga's done it for both men's and women's teams.

Georgia athletic teams take turns putting Uga on the cover of their media guides, but gymnastics coach Suzanne Yoculan takes it a step further. She has the mascot lead the team onto the floor for the first home meet every year, and Uga VI helped the Gym Dogs create this "Unleashed" poster (see p. 137).

Uga VI

Uga VI helped kick off the 2001-02 men's basketball season in Savannah, then appeared for pre-game warmups in the Coliseum prior to the Dogs' victory over Tennessee in January. Rules prevent the mascot from being on the floor during a game, but Uga VI managed to get his picture taken with Coach Jim Harrick just prior to tip-off.

Uga V was grand marshal of the 1998 Homecoming parade, and here Uga VI makes his debut parade appearance in October 1999.

Uga VI

You never know where the mascot will turn up next. Here, Uga VI helps president Michael Adams dedicate the university's new Baxter Street Esplanade, and poses with Georgia Speaker of the House Tom Murphy at a legislative reception in Atlanta.

Uga gets into and (with help) out of trouble

When Georgia played Kentucky in Lexington on Oct. 21, 2000, the football team was staying at the Marriott Griffin Gate. On the day before the game, Swann Seiler had Uga VI on the leash, having just taken him for a walk. As she neared the hotel elevator, she struck up a conversation with Tom Landrum, chief of staff to UGA president Michael Adams, Tom's wife Susan, and her mother, Nell Brown.

"Uga knows what an elevator's for," says Swann, "and when the door opened he got on—with me still holding his leash!"

As the door began to close, Tom Landrum realized the danger and jammed his hand between the doors to prevent them from closing all the way. They stayed open a few inches—but would not re-open.

"I was scared to death that the leash would get caught in the elevator door and choke Uga," says Swann, "but Tom's quick thinking gave me time to stuff the leash through the narrow crack between the elevator doors."

Landrum had no choice at that point but to let go of the doors, which closed—and away went Uga VI on a solo joyride.

"Can you imagine the look on people's faces!" Sonny would say afterward, "if the door to a party room had been left open and in walks Uga out for a night on the town! We hadn't given him a curfew. There's no telling when he would've come home—or what shape he would've been in!"

All kidding aside, the Seilers were really worried when the incident happened.

"We hadn't pushed the button to any floor, so we had no idea where Uga might get off," says Swann. "So we all ran up the stairs to different floors, hoping to find him."

When the elevator doors opened on the third floor, Uga VI walked straight into the waiting arms of Nell Brown, who showed remarkable speed for a woman in her seventies.

"Tom Landrum's title may be chief of staff to the president," says Sonny, "but he and Susan's mother are heroes to the Seilers."

How pervasive is the school mascot in University of Georgia culture? Well, UGA designer Rick Fiala was sufficiently inspired by Uga VI to create these "Warhol Bulldogs" for Food Services' 2000 calendar.

All Uga has to do is check into the Atlanta Hilton and the gossip columnists are all over it.

Sampling people chow in the skyboxes . . . or whose beef tenderloin is that?

Catered lunches are served in the Georgia skyboxes at home football games. The food is beautifully presented—and intended solely for humans. But don't tell that to Uga VI.

"We always take Uga to the skyboxes at halftime," says Sonny. "It's a good place for him to cool off, and we like to give Georgia fans a chance to see the mascot and get their photo taken with him."

Early in the 2001 season, the Seilers were walking Uga VI down the hall to the UGA Alumni Association box at the same time a caterer was pushing a stainless steel food cart down the hall to serve lunch. The hall was crowded and the caterer had to stop briefly to turn into a skybox. On the lower shelf of the cart was a pan of beef tenderloin with a demi-glaze sauce. As luck would have it, the pan happened to be dead-even with Uga VI's head—and when the cart stopped, he did what any red-blooded American dog would do when presented with such an inviting luncheon opportunity:

He stuck his head inside the stainless steel cart and helped himself to the beef tenderloin.

The caterer scolded Uga and pushed him away. Too late! Uga already had a mouthful of medium-rare beef with gravy dripping from his massive chin.

"Without hesitating," says Sonny, "the caterer smoothed over the remaining contents of the pan and pushed the cart into a skybox filled with hungry guests. We won't tell which skybox."

Set of wheels for the mascot

Uga IV loved his red wheelbarrow, but being a more modern dog, Uga VI has a more expensive plaything.

"Uga VI has never played Augusta National . . . I think it's a bit long for him, particularly now," says Sonny, who attends The Masters every year. "But thanks to the generosity of Rusty McGahee and the E-Z-GO company of Augusta, Uga VI does have his own Georgia-red golf cart."

Uga's new ride came equipped with headlights, horn, radio, fan, hard top, and a mini truck platform on the back—making it the perfect vehicle for transporting a dog with short legs from the back porch of the Seilers' new home near the Savannah Yacht Club down to their dock, where the family boat, "Silver Britches," is moored. To personalize the golf cart the way a famous athlete would personalize a new set of wheels, the Seilers added an Uga VI license tag to the back and an oval "G" to the front.

"You better believe Uga knows that's *his* golf cart!" says Cecelia. "We park it right next to his doggie condo in the garage, and it's impossible for Sonny and me to take a ride in it without Uga demanding to ride along. If he's in the backyard and he hears the beeper when we back it out, he comes a-running. If he's in the house, he will bark and carry on until you open the back door. And, ooooh Lordy, does he come flying at that thing!"

"Uga IV used to treat his wheelbarrow like a tackling dummy, and Uga VI comes at his golf cart the same way," says Sonny. "But he manages to slow down just enough to land safely on the floor of the cart . . . kind of like a UGA student flinging himself into a friend's car on Baldwin Street between classes. This has been a wonderful gift because it allows us to take Uga VI on rides around the neighborhood and to the yacht club. As you pass by people, you can hear them say, 'That's Uga's golf cart.'"

Uga VI is not a golfer. But thanks to Rusty McGahee and the E-Z-GO company of Augusta, he can ride around the Seilers' neighborhood or down to the boat dock in his very own customized golf cart.

Uga VI

Bulldogs are a way of life for the Dooleys

Vince Dooley grew up in Mobile and his undergraduate degree came from Auburn, where he distinguished himself as a player and got his first college coaching experience. But Dooley and his wife Barbara are about to celebrate their fortieth year at the University of Georgia, and one way to measure their allegiance to their adopted alma mater would be to count the number of bulldog statues, figurines, salt-and-pepper shakers, photos, and paintings they own.

"You could try, but you're bound to lose count—even we don't know how many we have," says Vince, whose home and office are shrines to the mascot. (Yes, that's him with little Uga V on p. 99.)

Beginning at the rear of the Dooleys' Five Points home, which is party central on Georgia football weekends, the pool house is guarded by an imposing wooden bulldog that was hand-carved to resemble an Indian totem pole. Guests entering the house from the patio area pass between two imposing bulldog statues. On the way to the den, visitors invariably stop at two curiosity pieces—a bulldog clock with a wagging tongue that functions as a second hand, and "The Butler Did It" statue of a bulldog serving champagne on a tray. Floor-to-ceiling bookcases are filled to overflowing with bulldog statues and figurines, including several from Georgia Crown chairman Don Leebern that double as flasks or mini decanters.

"We have so many," says Barbara, "that over the years they've spilled off the shelves and onto the floor—like litters of puppies. But we love them and they've a real conversation piece for our guests."

Vince Dooley's office on the fourth floor of the Butts-Mehre building isn't a whole lot different, beginning with a large

Vince Dooley (shown here with Uga III) can trace his tenure at Georgia all the way back to Uga I, who was the mascot when Dooley was hired as head coach in 1964.

oil painting of Uga I that has hung on the wall of his various offices since 1966.

"I called Lamar Dodd," says Dooley, "and told him I would like a painting of Uga for my wall, something that would reflect his proud history as mascot."

Dodd considered doing the painting himself, but recommended the late Walter Frobos, who was an experienced portrait artist.

"Walter studied a number of champion bulldogs, as well as Uga I," says Dooley. "What he came up with was this powerful rendering of Uga with that determined look in his eye . . . like he's saying to an opponent, 'I'm linin' up on defense. Now come on! I'm ready for you!'"

Asked to explain Uga's appeal with the Bulldog Nation, Dooley looks to Frobus' painting as though he were doing research for a master's thesis in history.

"Uga has this unique ability to appeal to young and old alike," says Dooley. "To the young, he's a lovable animal they instinctively trust and want to hug. I can attest to that because of something that happened when we were in Nashville for the 2001 Music City Bowl. One of my grandchildren had just had an unfortunate experience with a Lab. The dog wasn't vicious; I think my grandchild just got in his face and, for one reason or another, the dog nipped him. My grandchild had to get stitches and his face just looked awful. Okay, so now it's the next day and we're in the hotel and here comes Uga VI waddling across the lobby. With no hesitation whatsoever, my grandchild races right up to Uga and hugs him like he never had the run-in with the other dog! He wasn't a bit afraid of Uga!"

Older folks—particularly those who bleed red and black and live and die with

The late Walter Frobos painted this portrait of Uga I that hangs on the wall of Dooley's office. Dooley likes the determined look in Uga I's eye—like he's saying to an opponent, "I'm lining up on defense. Now come on! I'm ready for you!"

Uga VI

Georgia on the athletic field—identify with Uga in a different way, says Dooley.

Uga is symbolic of all those things you've come to know and respect about bulldogs—that relentless tenacity that you want your athletic teams to have. He leads our football team out onto the field, he's a fixture in our post-game locker room, he makes appearances for any Georgia athletic team that invites him . . . Uga is just inseparable from Georgia athletes. He's one of us!"

Georgia football players are so used to having Uga around, they just expect him to be there.

"I guess you could say our football players are a bit spoiled when it comes to Uga," says Dooley. "But I wish every loyal Bulldog fan could have seen our baseball team after they won the SEC championship in 2001. We had a press conference at Foley Field prior to their trip to the College World Series in Omaha, and the players were acting cool, calm, and collected—until Uga VI walked in to pose for some pictures with them—and then they turned into little kids. They got down on the floor with Uga—nose to nose with him—and a few of them even wrassled a little bit with him, I think. These young men were longing for some kind of big-league affirmation for what they'd accomplished—and Uga VI gave it to them big-time. They just kept saying, 'This is awesome!'"

For someone who can talk for hours about bulldogs of all makes and models—human, canine, ceramic, stone, and wooden—Dooley has never owned the real, live kind. He can't explain why,

The Dooleys' bulldog statues are so lifelike that visitors instinctively reach down and pet them.

but the reason may lie in not wanting to get so close that a bulldog would become just a dog, as opposed to Uga, who enjoys a somewhat mythic persona in Dooley's mind.

"We got a dog in 1980," he recalls. "It was a black Lab and the kids were trying to think of a name for him when I left with the team for the Tennessee game in Knoxville. You know what happened up there—the beginning of the Herschel Walker legend. So when I got home, the kids came rushing up to tell me they had thought of the perfect name for their new Lab puppy: Herschel. I said, 'Now, wait a minute, kids. We can't do that without asking the real Herschel.' So I did, and Herschel said, 'I'd be proud, Coach!' From then on, whenever I'd see ole No. 34, he'd say, 'How's Herschel doing, Coach?' And I'd say, 'Thanks for asking about Herschel, Herschel. He's doing just fine!'"

Herschel the Lab sired several litters in his fifteen years with the Dooleys, including a puppy named Catfish who was adopted—and later immortalized in prose—by the late humorist and UGA favorite son Lewis Grizzard.

"I am a dog lover, no question," says Dooley. "But Uga is more than just a dog. He brings new meaning to the word *mascot*. For proof, I refer you to the Savannah premiere of *Midnight in the Garden of Good and Evil,* which I attended. Movie stars like Kevin Spacey are getting all this applause as they walk down the red carpet. And now here comes Uga V . . . in a big limousine. When he got out of that limo and people saw him in his little black tuxedo, they went nuts! I think he got the loudest applause of anyone."

Vince Dooley is such a fan of the mascot that he couldn't resist getting his photo taken with Uga VI at Picture Day 2001.

Uga VI

The little girl's face is red, Uga V is panting heavily, and that was the problem with Picture Day when it was held outdoors in August heat. The athletic department solved the problem by moving indoors to the air-conditioned comfort of the Classic Center in downtown Athens.

Uga VI

Fans like to come by the Seilers' SUV prior to kickoff to get their picture taken with Uga—or just to pat him for good luck.

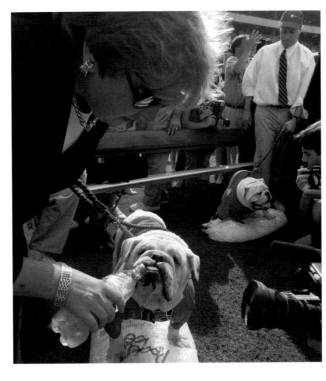

The easiest way to keep the mascots cool during warm-weather appearances is for them to drink bottled water, so Georgia Crown chairman and UGA alumnus Don Leebern keeps them well supplied with his Melwood Springs brand. Here, Swann cools off Uga V at the '99 changing-of-the-collar ceremony.

Swann: Master of the thirty-second photo-op

It's a Friday afternoon at Savannah Electric's offices on the Riverfront, and manager of corporate communications Swann Seiler has just been asked for a thumbnail description of her duties at the company. She rattles off "public and community relations, advertising and media relations, special events, and executive support."

And that's just what she does from nine-to-five. At lunch, at night, and on weekends, Swann also has found time to serve as president of the Junior League, president of the Girl Scouts, and chair of Savannah's United Way Campaign.

Asked where she gets all that initiative, Swann replies, without hesitation: "Everyone in my family is a workaholic."

Expected to earn her own spending money as a kid—as were all the Seiler children—Swann had summer jobs, Christmas vacation jobs, babysitting jobs, day camp jobs, ice cream scoop jobs.

"You name it and I did it," says Swann, whose work ethic with regard to Uga has manifested itself in a number of ways over the years—chief among them being her role as a photo setup person on Picture Day in August and at the Seilers' SUV prior to kickoff on football Saturdays.

"Swann is good with people and good with Uga," says Sonny. "You see that when she has to be the go-between at Picture Day, getting hundreds of people a thirty-second photo-op with Uga—many of them with little children and babies and cameras that won't flash. Without Swann, Picture Day would be a total disaster because a lot of people just freeze when they get near Uga. They're like kids with Santa. They forget what to do."

Fortunately, Uga never forgets what to do—namely, to be patient and affectionate with anyone Swann puts next to him.

"These dogs are so gentle that we never worry about them on Picture Day, regardless of how much people want to pet, hug, or even kiss Uga while getting their picture taken," says Swann. "In a rare case, a young child may scream or cry, but Uga pays it no mind. He's just happy to be with people."

Picture Day is always held in August, and in years past it was held at the UGA practice field. A covered shed offered some relief from the late summer heat, but the artificial turf radiated it back up at Uga and Swann and the Bulldog faithful waiting in line for their photo with Uga. The athletic department solved the problem by moving Picture Day indoors to the air-conditioned comfort of the Classic Center.

On football Saturdays in the fall, Uga makes a number of appearances on behalf of the university.

"If it's Homecoming," says Swann, "we might make stops at receptions for the vet school and business school, plus a law school picnic and an interview with the journalism students' University

Uga VI

News show. If there's a swim meet or a soccer or volleyball match, Daddy has us stop by there, too. By game time, we're pooped!"

The Seilers park their SUV under the bridge at the west end of Sanford Stadium, and they like to keep Uga there as long as possible prior to kickoff. He's comfortable in his carrier and the car air-conditioner keeps him relatively cool. But Swann can't relax yet because the Seilers open the tailgate of the SUV to allow fans to lean in next to Uga and snap a quick photo.

"Some people just want to pat his head or say hello to him on the way to their seats," says Swann, "and you'd be surprised how many of those people are wearing Tech or Auburn hats. Everybody loves Uga—but particularly the young kids."

If all parties cooperate, this is what the before and after should look like, as ten-month-old Miller McGee of Marietta shows his affection for Uga VI at Picture Day 2001.

to get to the field," says Swann, "and as these players are moving through the tunnel, a couple of Vandy recruits catch sight of Uga —and want their picture taken with him. He's a hero to both sides!"

The other Nashville story features Swann and Uga:

"I get in bed on Friday night before the game and, as is typical of Uga VI, he comes over to my bed and licks my ear, hoping I'll want to play. I don't, so I lay perfectly still so he'll think I'm asleep. He leaves me alone and I fall

Swann can give you chapter and verse on all six of the dogs, and a couple of her favorite stories about Uga took place in Nashville. The first one was told to her by Georgia's director of football operations, Steve Greer, who was a member of the coaching staff when it happened.

"Both the Georgia and Vanderbilt teams use the same tunnel

asleep thinking everything's fine. But Uga VI is fond of making things his own—even things that don't belong to him. And when I wake up in the morning, the room is a complete mess! He has taken every article of clothing out of my suitcase and scattered them, one by one, all over the room . . . and he did it so quietly that I didn't hear a thing!"

Uga poses with hundreds of people on Picture Day, but he is so gentle and affectionate—particularly with children—that the Seilers never worry about his manners.

Uga VI

room, if you're not watching him closely he'll grab a roll of toilet paper and chew it to pieces—or eat the soap!"

Charles has been the mascots' principal handler since he was fourteen years old. On game days, he takes charge of Uga just prior to kickoff and, except for a brief handoff to the cheerleaders for the team run-on, he stays on duty until Sonny takes Uga to the post-game lockerroom—where, as Sonny says, "the mascots are sworn never to divulge what they hear." Sonny returns Uga to the Seilers' SUV after the game—where still more people gather for more picture-taking.

The most frequent question Charles gets during his sideline duty is "Why does he lie on that bag of ice?"

Standard answer: "Because he's hot."

When film crews or still photographers want an environmental portrait of Uga—which happens several times a game—Charles has to lift the sixty-pound dog onto the cheerleaders' platform, and hold him steady during the picture-taking. To put it bluntly, he is used to having a dog's butt in his face—and used to being cropped out of most of the photos taken of Uga.

"My *hands* have been in *Sports Illustrated* four times," says Charles. "That's the extent of my celebrity."

Charles: The unsung hero

Charles Seiler's earliest memories of Uga have nothing to do with him being a famous school mascot; Charles related to him as any young boy would relate to his dog. Every day was an adventure. When Uga III got out of the family yard on Forty-fourth Street in Savannah—which happened a good bit—Charles would yell, "Dog escape!" and he and his sisters would give chase.

"As we were trying to catch him," says Charles, who is now in the bond business with Palmer & Cay in Savannah, "we'd see kids climbing trees to escape the runaway dog. They were afraid of Uga, which we thought was funny."

Like Swann, Charles has vivid memories of the dogs, beginning with Uga III, and he doesn't hesitate to classify Uga VI as the most rambunctious.

"He hasn't shaken the puppy in him yet," says Charles, "and he can be a real pain in the butt. When we check into a hotel

On game days, Charles works as hard as any of the UGA trainers. But he gets cropped out of many Uga photos.

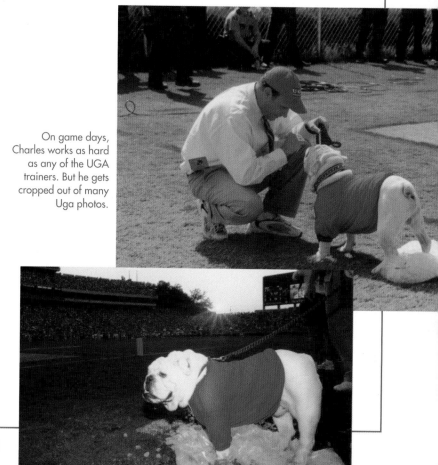

146

Cecelia: Best mum an English bull could have

When the Seilers take Uga to Athens for a football game, Cecelia is behind the wheel. When Uga has to go to the vet, Cecelia makes the appointment and delivers him there and back. When he needs a bath, Cecelia puts him in the tub and gives him a good scrubbing. Time to eat? Yep, Cecelia's the one filling the bowl.

"These dogs require a lot of attention and care," says Cecelia, "but it's like I've said before—we got Uga I before I had my first child and they've been a fixture in our lives ever since."

Uga VI

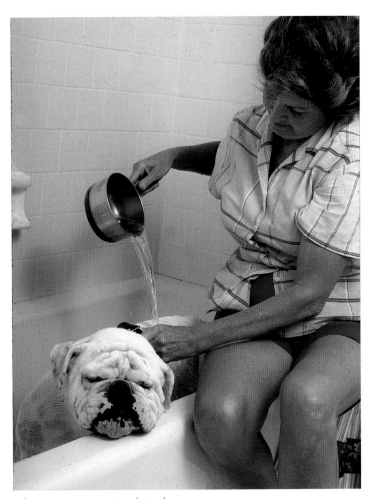

When it comes to Uga, Cecelia's job description includes everything from bath time to trips to the vet.

The den of the Seilers' former home on Dutch Island doubled as an Uga museum. That's Uga IV with Cecelia.

Uga VI

"All he's got to know how to do is walk and run. If I said, 'Uga, sit' or 'roll over,' or 'play dead,' uh-uh. Uga doesn't do tricks."

—Cecelia Seiler

In family photos—or at a student photo day on Herty Field—Cecelia is the one holding the leash.

Cecelia's children are all grown and on their own, but Uga provides long-term protection against Empty Nest Syndrome.

Sonny: Keeper of the flame

Vince Dooley says the applause Uga gets at occasions like the *Midnight* premiere should also be directed at the Seilers—and particularly at Sonny, because he has energized the whole mascot thing from day one.

"Sonny is . . . well, *Sonny* . . . you could write volumes about him," says Dooley. "One of the most remarkable things about him is his attention to detail. The letters I've gotten from him over the years—telling me they've moved Otto's grave to their new home and he knew I'd want to know, sending me newspaper clippings that promote Georgia in a positive way, congratulating us on recruiting, keeping me abreast of Uga's schedule—you could start a library with them! Thank God, he's writing a book!

A MAN & HIS DOG.

PHOTO BY: TRAVIS ELLISON

Uga VI

"What's so heart-warming about Sonny," Dooley adds, "is that he's an old-fashioned Southern gentleman who stands on ceremony—and he always wants my approval on things. But the truth is, I have so much trust and faith in him that, when it comes to the mascots, he doesn't need my approval because I know he's going to do the right thing. They don't come any more loyal than Sonny. I don't think we've got a greater promoter of the University of Georgia than Sonny—and, oh my, has he trained his family well. Cecelia, Swann, Charles, Bess, and Sara . . . there's no doubt what they hold dear and what they're prepared to sacrifice for Georgia. And they've been doing it for almost a half-century now."

"The thing I can't figure out," says Sonny, "is how much older I look now than when I started. Whereas, Uga doesn't seem to have aged a day."

President Adams says the mascots are the rallying point of the Bulldog Nation.

Uga VI

Presidential seal of approval

Vince Dooley's memories of the Uga dynasty precede his being hired as Georgia football coach in 1964, and Michael Adams got acquainted with Uga VI even before he was named president of the University of Georgia in 1997.

"I don't know how Uga is as smart as he is," says Adams, who is sipping coffee in his office on North Campus. "But before I had been announced as president, that photograph of him you see on my wall arrived in the mail. It had Uga's paw print on it and an inscription from him addressing me as 'Boss Man.' So, literally, from before my first day in office, my first communication from UGA—other than the presidential search committee, which Sonny was a member of—came from Uga. That's how efficiently Uga operates."

In Adams' first five years as president, he has gotten to know the Seilers so well that Uga and the Adams' dog, Casey, exchange Christmas gifts.

"I can't even begin to describe what Sonny and Cecelia and Swann and Charles mean to the University of Georgia—and to Mary and me," says Adams. "Their only motivation is to give.

They are the most selfless people I know. What they provide the university is an invaluable service—and they've never even asked for expenses.

"I have stood with them in freezing cold in Nashville, in pouring rain in Knoxville, and in blistering heat in Jacksonville —and I've never seen them even appear not to be enjoying it. They are a remarkable family, and the emotions tied to this relationship—between this dog and his family and their alma mater—are truly unprecedented."

When Adams says Uga is special, he speaks from experience. He has years of NCAA committee work under his belt, and at each one of his stops in higher education, as a student, faculty member, and administrator, he was aware of the impact a mascot can have on school spirit. He got his undergraduate degree from Lipscomb University (Bison) in Nashville and his master's and doctorate in political communications from Ohio State (Buckeyes). He was a high-ranking administrator at Pepperdine (The Wave) before becoming president of Centre College (Colonels) in Kentucky. All of those schools had athletic mascots, but in Adams' estimation none of them holds a candle to Uga.

"We had a dressed-up Wave at Pepperdine that, to be honest,

Uga and beauty queens: photographers can't get enough of them.

Uga VI

"On one level, you think before you go, *Is this a bit trivial?*" says Adams. "But Mary told me that once she got there, she really felt like a member of the family had passed away. Clearly, you don't want to equate the importance of a canine with a person—and yet, this dog symbolizes something that's larger than life."

And Uga VI has picked up where Uga V left off.

"I entertained 150 guests at the 2001 Music City Bowl in Nashville," says Adams. "At the pre-game luncheon we set up an arrangement sort of like Santa Claus where our guests—many of whom are captains of industry—could sit in a chair next to Uga and have their photo taken with him. I can't tell you how excited those people were. You could tell by the looks on their faces and by the thank-you letters I received afterward."

Kathy Pulliam, a senior administrative secretary in the president's office, has a good reason for using Uga as a screensaver on her computer. Over the years, the Seilers have made a habit of stopping at her father's gas station and country store in Glascock County on the way from Savannah to Athens.

looked like a Smurf," says Adams. "I love Ohio State, but their Hairy Dawg counterpart, Brutus Buckeye, is definitely not Uga. And the Kentucky Colonel at Centre looked like Colonel Sanders. So there is a real advantage to having a living, breathing mascot who can make appearances, as Uga does. Plus, we are a nation of dog-lovers and football fans—and Uga looks like a middle linebacker! There's a certain power in that, but what I really like and respect about Uga is his quiet strength. You don't want to wax overly poetic about a dog. But there's grace and strength and tradition in Uga VI as he stands on the sidelines, connected to nearly a half-century of his predecessors who are buried nearby in the southwest corner of the stadium. Uga is the centerpiece and the rallying point of the Bulldog Nation."

When Uga V died, Adams was out of town and his wife Mary attended the funeral.

President Adams, Cecelia, and Mary Adams at the 2001 Music City Bowl in Nashville.

Media star

ESPN sideline reporter Adrian Karsten seconds Adams' opinion that Uga trumps everyone else's mascot.

"Uga does more to help his team and his school than any of the other tigers, birds, or insects," says Karsten. "And he's got a presence about him that even coaches and players recognize. When he runs the team onto the field at the start of the game, the coaches actually hold the players back at about the 20-yard line so they don't upstage Uga."

Karsten has done a number of different features on Uga over the years, but says he has something special in mind for Uga VI.

"No broadcaster has gotten *inside* that air-conditioned doghouse," says the 6'7" Karsten, who admits it would be a tight squeeze. "With a dog of Uga's stature, you don't just invite yourself in—but it's something I'd love to do some day."

Uga VI continues a tradition of service to UGA by doing both commercial and institutional ads that benefit the university. If you look closely at the "Get your house in order" ad, you can see the air-conditioning unit in the back of Uga's doghouse.

Uga VI

First Family of UGA Athletics

In April, as the academic year is coming to an end and student-athletes are getting ready to graduate or head home for the summer, the UGA Athletic Association holds a day-long staff retreat at the Georgia Center for Continuing Education.

"It's a good time for us to assess where we've been and where we're going," says athletic director Vince Dooley. "It's also a time for us to assess what we've achieved during the past year and, to recognize those staff members who have made it possible for us to win conference and NCAA championships."

The guest speaker at the athletic association's 2002 "Mission Renewal Day" was then-Southeastern Conference commissioner Roy Kramer, who opened his remarks with a tribute to Uga.

"The first time I came to Athens for a football game when I was athletic director at Vanderbilt, I pulled into the Georgia Center and, amazingly, found a parking place," said Kramer. "I checked in and took my suitcase to the room. Fifteen minutes later, a young man knocked on my door and told me I'd have to move my car—because I was in the mascot's spot and Uga was on his way to Athens. I had to park my car a half-mile away and walk back to the Georgia Center. That's how I learned the true significance of the Georgia Bulldog!"

Uga VI

President Adams says of the Seilers, "I have stood with them in freezing cold in Nashville, and in blistering heat in Jacksonville—and I've never seen them even appear not to be enjoying it."

When a dog graces the cover of *Sports Illustrated* and does all the things Uga does for the University of Georgia, it's not surprising that he commands his own parking place—or that his family is honored for making it all possible. That was the case at the athletic association's retreat, where the First Family of UGA Athletics—the Seilers of Savannah—received the Bill Powell Award for meritorious service (see photo below).

When all the speeches had been made and all the awards given out, Vince Dooley asked that the lights in Masters Hall be dimmed for a slide show commemorating a year when Georgia would finish eighth in the annual Sears Cup competition for best overall collegiate athletic program in the country. But no athletes were shown. Instead, staff members saw photos of only themselves:

The Seilers were recently honored with a special service award from the UGA Athletic Association to go with one they had already received from the UGA Alumni Association. The award is named for former faculty athletics representative Bill Powell (at left).

Trainers working in the whirlpool room. Publicity people logging information into a computer. Stadium and grounds personnel toiling outdoors in the heat. Secretaries keeping the office humming. Coaches doing their thing. Custodians making sure everything is ship-shape.

It takes 250 full-time athletic staff members to make NCAA and SEC championships possible, and the man singled out as the 2000 Employee of the Year was Jack Ollie, a utility worker who was hired by the athletic association way back in 1962—when Vince Dooley was still at Auburn. Ollie received a special plaque honoring him for forty years of faithful service to the athletic association.

But there is one ex-officio employee of the athletic association who predates both Ollie and Dooley. With the rock anthem "We Are the Champions" bringing "Mission Renewal Day" and the slide show to a close, one final image appeared on the screen. It was a photo of Uga—and the room erupted in applause.

Special University of Georgia
Guests in Attendance

UGA VI
Escorted by Sonny and Cecelia Seiler

Vince Dooley
Athletic Director

Mark Richt
Head Football Coach

Steve Wrigley
⋯ior Vice President for External Affairs

RSVP by July 8
Business Attire

/706)542-7619
vpuga@uga.edu

The honored guests listed on this invitation to a congressional reception in Washington included Georgia athletic director Vince Dooley and head football coach Mark Richt. But the name at the top of the invitation was Uga VI.

Uga goes to Washington

The invitation came from the top, with UGA president Michael Adams inviting D.C.-area alumni to attend a special reception to recognize members of the Georgia congressional delegation for their support of the University of Georgia. But above Adams' name—at the very top of the invitation, under the heading "Special University of Georgia Guests in Attendance" and ahead of Vince Dooley, football coach Mark Richt, and UGA senior vice president Steve Wrigley—was Uga VI, headlining the whole shebang.

And that's the way the press played the story.

The *Savannah Morning News* previewed Uga VI's trip to Washington with a feature story that ran on the front page of the Sunday edition. The story began: "Move over Armey and Gephardt. Watch out Daschle and Lott. Tuesday evening there will be a new top dog on Capitol Hill."

And that's pretty much what happened.

On Tuesday morning, July 16, 2002, a private plane picked up Sonny, Cecelia, and Uga VI at the Savannah Airport. The eight-passenger, twin-engine aircraft made a midday stop in Athens to pick up a UGA contingent that included Dooley and Richt, and alumni association president Carlton Curtis, who is a vice president for Coca-Cola's North American division. By late afternoon, the UGA charter had landed at Dulles Airport outside D.C., where an air-conditioned van was waiting to transport the entourage to the district.

"We pull into the parking lot at the Russell Senate Building," says Sonny, "and it's a mob scene . . . photographers everywhere, snapping pictures of Uga like he was running for office!"

The Seilers walked Uga through the security checkpoint and took the elevator to the second floor. The big fella needed a few minutes to cool off, so Sonny and Cecelia walked him down the hall, gave him a drink of water, and let him relax on the cool marble floor for a few minutes. There was the usual struggle to

get Uga VI into his red Georgia jersey, and then it was show time.

"The reception is in the Senate Caucus Room, where the Watergate hearings were held," says Sonny. "A jazz combo is playing and when Uga walks in, 300 people—senators and congressmen included—burst into spontaneous applause! Cecelia and I are thinking, *Well, here we are . . . a typical Wednesday evening with Uga.*"

One by one and two by two, distinguished elected officials, their staff members, and D.C.-area alumni came forward to have

Uga VI

UGA invited to D.C.

Mascot will be honored guest at reception for university alumni serving in Congress.

By Jenel Few
Savannah Morning News

Move over Armey and Gephardt. Watch out Daschle and Lott. Tuesday evening there will be a new top dog on Capitol Hill.

The University of Georgia is holding a reception in the Russell Senate Office Building for the Georgia Congressional Delegation and the congressional leaders and staff who are alumni of the institution.

The guest of honor is UGA VI.

see UGA, page 6A

UGA IV
Read about his political history on Page 6A.

The *Savannah Morning News* previewed Uga VI's trip to Washington on the front page of its Sunday edition.

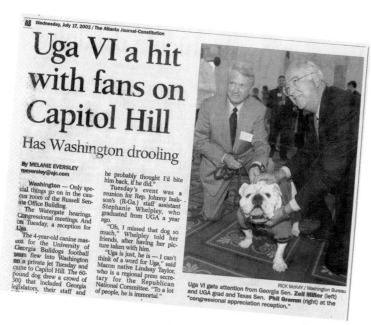

AS Wednesday, July 17, 2002 / The Atlanta Journal-Constitution

Uga VI a hit with fans on Capitol Hill

Has Washington drooling

By MELANIE EVERSLEY
meversley@ajc.com

Washington — Only special things go on in the caucus room of the Russell Senate Office Building.

The Watergate hearings. Congressional meetings. And on Tuesday, a reception for Uga.

The 4-year-old canine mascot for the University of Georgia Bulldogs football team flew into Washington on a private jet Tuesday and came to Capitol Hill. The 60-pound dog drew a crowd of 300 that included Georgia legislators, their staff and

he probably thought I'd bite him back, if he did."

Tuesday's event was a reunion for Rep. Johnny Isakson's (R-Ga.) staff assistant Stephanie Whelpley, who graduated from UGA a year ago.

"Oh, I missed that dog so much," Whelpley told her friends, after having her picture taken with him.

"Uga is just, he is — I can't think of a word for Uga," said Macon native Lindsay Taylor, who is a regional press secretary for the Republican National Committee. "To a lot of people, he is immortal."

RICK McKAY / Washington Bureau
Uga VI gets attention from Georgia Sen. **Zell Miller** (left) and UGA grad and Texas Sen. **Phil Gramm** (right) at the "congressional appreciation reception."

Two of UGA's most loyal and successful graduates, U.S. senators Zell Miller (D-Georgia) and Phil Gramm (R-Texas) got their pictures taken with Uga VI at the congressional reception on July 16, 2002.

their pictures taken with Uga VI, who made himself available between bites of roast beef slipped to him by a loyal alum who was also responsible for creating the event.

Senators Zell Miller (D-Georgia) and Phil Gramm (R-Texas), both UGA grads, got down on one knee for their portrait with Uga. Said Gramm: "Uga was probably the best-looking one in the picture."

Throwing decorum to the wind, Representative Jack Kingston (R-Georgia), who hails from Savannah and has loved the Georgia mascots since he was a boy, got down on the floor of the caucus room and hugged Uga VI—just as Clint Eastwood had done in Sonny's law office the day he cast Uga V in the film version of *Midnight in the Garden of Good and Evil.*

This peculiar version of American pomp and circumstance struck a chord with editors of *The Guardian* in far-off London, England, who picked up the Associated Press story. Under *The Guardian* headline "Georgia Bulldog steals show in D.C." the story read:

"It was unlike most Washington receptions: senators and congressmen were there, but the celeb most in demand Tuesday was a panting short guy who flew up from Georgia in a private jet to be with his admirers. Uga VI, the bulldog with a fan base that tops any other representative of the University of Georgia, was in his element."

The Atlanta and Athens newspapers followed suit.

"Uga VI a hit with fans on Capitol Hill . . . Has Washington drooling," read the *Atlanta Journal-Constitution* headline.

"For a day, top dog king of the hill in D.C." noted the *Athens Banner-Herald.*

Both Dooley and Richt addressed the crowd at the Russell Senate Building, each happily admitting they were playing second fiddle.

"I know you came to see Uga," Richt acknowledged with a smile, "but I was glad to be able to coattail along."

"I've always been upstaged," said Dooley. "That was part of the contract when I arrived. I was always behind Uga. When Herschel won the Heisman Trophy, Uga was there. Each generation of Uga has its special moments."

This one was conceived by young Adil Durrani, who, while a student at UGA, never got to see Uga up close. Once, in the middle of the night, he and some friends sneaked into Sanford Stadium to get a close look at Uga's doghouse. But Durrani, who graduated from UGA in 2001, had never stood nose to jowl with

Uga VI

Uga VI's appearance in D.C. made headlines as far away as London. This photo was taken by filmmakers producing a documentary about Uga and the Seilers for Nowhere Productions in Athens.

Uga VI

Uga—until the congressional reception, that is. Durrani is now a staff assistant to Sen. Max Cleland (D-Georgia.), and his job description includes setting up special events. He admits to harboring a selfish motive with this one.

"It was definitely a special moment," Durrani told *AJC* writer Melanie Eversley of looking into Uga VI's grateful eyes while feeding him medium-rare treats. "I think I enjoyed feeding him roast beef because it was unique—and I thought he'd like me more."

"Oh, I missed that dog so much," said another '01 UGA graduate, Stephanie Whelpley, now a staff assistant to Representative Johnny Isakson (R-Georgia.).

"Uga is just . . . he is . . . I can't think of a word for Uga," said Macon native Lindsay Taylor, a regional press secretary for the Republican National Committee. "To a lot of people, he is immortal."

Immortal, perhaps—at least in the minds of Bulldog faithful. But he is definitely not perfect.

"He barked three times during the speeches," says Sonny. "But the crowd loved it when he acted like a regular dog. I think he wanted more of that roast beef!"

The one-day sojourn to D.C. prompted Richt to ask Sonny for a favor.

"I can't tell you how much I appreciate what you do for the football team," said Richt, who asked Sonny if it would be possible for Uga to pose with members of each year's recruiting class so those photos can be sent to moms and dads and hometown newspapers.

"Of course!" said Sonny, whose trip to the congressional reception reminded him of the political influence Uga could wield:

"Uga is, by necessity, bi-partisan. He has to be because the University of Georgia has so many elected officials on both sides of the aisle."

And friends even at rival schools. In 1972, for example, former Sen. Sam Nunn (D-Georgia) made a special campaign stop in Athens, where he and Uga walked a lap around Sanford Stadium to a standing ovation from the crowd (see photo on p. 51).

"The cheers were more for Uga," Sonny recalls, "but Sam got a lot of mileage out of it. And the irony of it all is that Sam Nunn went to Tech."

There's just something about this dog

Part of Uga's appeal—his mystique, if you will—is that he's a high-visibility dog with low exposure. High visibility in that the public sees his familiar, all-white countenance everywhere: magazine covers, TV, front page of the morning paper, movies, and, of course, football stadiums in the fall. And yet, low exposure because he keeps pretty much to himself when he's not toiling on behalf of the University of Georgia. Geography figures into it. Uga lives in Savannah, which means you're not going to see him out for a walk on Milledge Avenue in Athens during the week. But the Seilers are also careful not to commercialize the Uga road show.

"We've never even asked for a dealer courtesy car and you're not going to see Uga open a shopping center in Gwinnett because that's not the image we want for these dogs . . . their main mission is service," says Sonny. "When they make an appearance at a UGA swim meet or pose for a photo with the gymnastics team, they're there to work—and to add to the fun for Georgia fans. But when Uga's not on duty for the university, he's home in Savannah just being a dog . . . our family dog."

Uga lives near the Savannah Yacht Club on a cul-de-sac, which affords both him and the Seilers the privacy they lack when they're on duty. And despite his elevated stature in the dog world, Uga's accommodations in the Seilers' garage are nothing special. When you open the door, you know instantly if Uga's in his pen because his panting is so heavy it sounds like a car idling.

If Uga's not in his pen, you generally find him sacked out on the tiled floor of the Seilers' family room. Visitors make his body wiggle with anticipation because, in Uga's mind, there's always the chance they will want to: a.) play with me, b.) give me ice cream [preferably Breyer's vanilla], c.) take me for a ride in my golf cart, and so on.

When you enter the Seilers' family room, Uga instinctively grabs his special blanket and stares at you, hoping you will be foolish enough to try to steal it from him as he soars, Herschel-like, over the goal line to beat Notre Dame and win the National Championship. Actually, there is no goal line in the Seilers'

family room. Nor can Uga soar, in any way, shape, or form. But he can run with speed, power, and Herschel-like determination. Bottom line: If you decide to get down on the floor and play get-the-blankie with Uga, you better be prepared to break a sweat.

"These dogs . . . these wonderful English bulldogs . . . are not for the faint of heart," says Sonny. "But when you look at their wrinkled faces, there's just something about these dogs that makes you want to love them. Clearly, we feel that way because we have devoted our lives to them—and they, in turn, have been incredibly devoted to us."

And to the Bulldog Nation, says UGA Alumni Association director Dave Muia.

"Regardless of your class year, major, hometown, or GPA, Uga makes you feel part of this remarkable family," says Muia. "Through the years, he is the one constant you can count on seeing at UGA events. Administrators, faculty, students, athletes—they come and go. But Uga is always here."

People are attracted to that stability, says Sonny, and to something deeply personal that Uga awakens in those who went to school in Athens.

Here's an indication of how deeply ingrained bulldogs are in Sonny's life. He and alumni relations director Dave Muia are walking down a street in Assisi, Italy, on an alumni tour—and up walks a white bulldog who lives there in the ancient town. "He wasn't as big or as noble as Uga," says Sonny, "and his accent never would've gone over in Georgia."

Uga VI

Visitors are a welcome sight to Uga VI, who loves to play get-the-blankie on the floor of the Seilers' family room.

"As long as there's a University of Georgia . . . there will always be an Uga."

—Sonny Seiler

"When alumni look at Uga," says Sonny, "they see much more than a dog. They see the University of Georgia, which shaped their future. They also see their youth—which they're able to recapture, a part of it at least, every time they return to Athens. And they see an attitude . . . a tenacious, never-say-die will to succeed that rubs off on everybody who's around these Damn Good Dogs!

"As long as there's a University of Georgia, as long as there are UGA students, as long as there are devoted alumni and fans, as long as there's a Sanford Stadium and intercollegiatre athletics, as long as there is a sense of Bulldog tradition and pride . . . there will always be an Uga."

Uga VI

When people look at Uga, says Sonny, they see much more than a dog.
They see their alma mater—and they're reminded of college days in Athens.

How the Bulldog Got His Face

When the Good Lord gave out faces to the dogs long, long ago,
He found, when He had issued them there was still one dog to go.

"Where's this dog's face?" He called aloud. "I know I must have made it.
There must be someone here abouts who's clumsily mislaid it."

A shy young angel then stepped up, "Forgive me, Lord," he said.
He stuttered and he stammered and he turned a little red.

"I never thought it was a face—it fell out of your bag.
So I thought you had discarded it as just a piece of rag.

"So I promptly went and used it for very many things,
Like polishing up the halos and waxing up the wings.

"It's creased and crumpled as you see—in truth it's a disgrace.
I don't know how, my dearest Lord, you can use it for a face.

"I realize it's all my fault, and there's no one else to blame.
I trust you can forgive me, Lord, my heart's so full of shame."

"Of course I have forgiven you, but here we've got a mess,
so I'll make amends to this poor dog and him I'll truly bless.

"He'll be called an 'English Bulldog,' that's about the only place
where the people are so silly as to love an ugly face.

"But he'll be kind and gentle and of courage he'll be full—
As well as love and loyalty—the ugly, lovely Bull."

And that is how, my children, in that long gone year of grace
The dear old English Bulldog got his lovely ugly face.

—A.N.K. Hobbs

Uga VI

Is this the best dog in America? Georgia Bulldog fans obviously think so. For proof, we offer this portrait—commissioned by no less an expert than Eastman Kodak—which was used in a huge "Capture the Moment!" ad that greeted arriving passengers at Atlanta's Hartsfield Airport. "When people looked up at the Kodak ad says Sonny Seiler, "I know what they were thinking: *That's a damn good dog!*"

Acknowledgments

My first collaboration with Sonny Seiler was on a cover story for *Georgia Magazine*. "Uga goes to Hollywood!" was a behind-the-scenes look at *Midnight in the Garden of Good and Evil* from the viewpoint of Sonny and Uga V, both of whom had roles in the film version of John Berendt's blockbuster bestseller. I can't remember how it came up, but as Sonny was giving me a walking tour of Mercer House and some of the other *Midnight* landmarks in Savannah, we decided to do a book about Uga. The conversation lasted maybe thirty seconds, but it triggered more than two years of research and writing—and ultimately the birth of *Damn Good Dogs!*

A book that recounts this much oral and pictorial history, through six dogs and nearly a half-century of mascot duty, would have been impossible if Sonny and his wife Cecelia hadn't saved every important element of the Uga saga as though it were evidence in one of Sonny's legal cases. From Uga I's 1956 student ID card and the Bible he chewed up when the family went to the drive-in movie without him to Christmas cards of Uga VI on his red golf cart, the Seilers' array of photos and Uga memorabilia is so plentiful—and tells such wonderful stories about the University of Georgia and the Bulldog Nation—that the UGA Library has staked its claim to the collection whenever Sonny and Cecelia can bear to part with it.

We found more Uga photos in UGA's sports communications office in Athens. Some had been donated by Sonny and the rest had either been shot on behalf of the athletic department or donated by photographers who treat Uga more like a celebrity with each passing year. We thank the photographers for helping us bring Uga's story to life and Claude Felton's sports communication staff—in particular, Karen Huff, Karlene Lawrence, and Jenn Garrett—for helping us check facts and figures. We are also indebted to their ultimate boss, athletic director Vince Dooley, who is one of the main characters in this book, owing to the fact that he was hired as head football coach at Georgia in 1964, when the patriarch of the mascot line, Uga I, was still on duty. We also tip our hat to the man who, eight years earlier, convinced Coach Wally Butts that Uga I ought to be UGA's official school mascot: Dan Magill.

What we couldn't find in either Sonny's or Claude's photo files, we got from a number of sources, but we are especially indebted to Rick O'Quinn and UGA Photographic Services and to John Curry and the *Athens Banner-Herald.*

Having interviewed hundreds of witnesses over the years, Sonny got *Damn Good Dogs!* rolling by interviewing himself. Holed up at his beach house on Tybee Island, he spent four months rummaging through boxes of files and organizing the contents, and then long weekends dictating his version of the saga into a tape recorder. Sonny's legal secretary Mary Nagel painstakingly transcribed The Uga Tapes, which were proofread by the Seilers' dear friend Nancy Elliott Lee, who has been correcting Sonny since high school.

Memories come from places other than dusty file boxes, and this book would not have been complete (or as much fun!) without the contributions of the Seilers' four children—Swann, Charles, Bess, and Sara—who grew up with the dogs and who remembered things Sonny and Cecelia had forgotten. Or that they never knew—like the children playing hide-and-seek with Uga in the corridors of the Georgia Center when their parents went out to dinner.

Sonny is also grateful to UGA promotions director Avery McLean, who handles the merchandising of the mascot; to Bulldog Club secretary Loran Smith, for convincing him over the years that he ought to write a book about Uga; and to the UGA College of Veterinary Medicine, for providing the dogs with expert medical care.

As the chapters emerged from my computer, a number of people lent valuable assistance in the areas of research, proofreading, photography, and photo-scanning. Heading that list is my in-house editorial adviser and UGA information source Sharron Hannon, whom I adore and who teaches me something new every day. Other contributors who deserve thanks include Jan Beckley, Cheri Wranosky, Rebecca Reid, Steve Davis, Rachel Smith, Jeff Holman, Beth Tamboli, and Joëlle Prine.

I did a lot of the initial photo scanning myself, which would not have been possible if the person who got me interested in writing to begin with—former English teacher turned sorority housemother Mary Alice Hannon—hadn't bought me an Epson 2450. Thanks, Mom! You, too, Dad, for lots of things, including that telegram you sent me at Purdue. And I would be remiss if I didn't pay tribute to my incredible kids, Shane and Blake, and daughter-in-law Terra. Thanks, guys . . . the cheerleading kept me going!

Sonny and I are pleased that this book is being done by an Athens publisher with offices directly across the street from the Arch, and we have enjoyed working with the good people of Hill Street Press: Anne Boston, Judy Long, Tom Payton, and Gabriel Wilmoth.

To all those people whose lives have intersected with the Seilers' and who have shared their memories of Uga with us—people whose names appear in that long list in the index—Sonny and I offer our heartfelt thanks.

And to the person who holds this book in their hands . . . we hope you enjoy reading *Damn Good Dogs!* as much as we did writing it!

—Kent Hannon

Photo Credits

Arby's	Program ad (5)
Armstrong State	Uga V's honorary degree (5)
Athens Newspapers	Uga VI w/Hairy Dawg (Prologue); ribbed jersey (1); fireplug clip, (2); Uga III funeral (3); puppy w/hat (4); *Athens Magazine* cover, Uga lick, Uga Cam clip (5); cheerleaders lead Uga VI, Swann watering Uga V, Picture Day shots (6)
Atlanta Journal-Constitution	Butch clip, ferocious bulldog clip, Butts cover, Trouble? clip, Sapp, coaches shake hands (1); Baldy cartoon (3); Peach Buzz, D.C. clip (6)
Brian Boyd	Film crew on turf (5)
Carrette Studios	Sonny w/Jack Thompson (5)
Coca-Cola North America	"Georgia Favorites" ad (Prologue)
Columbus Ledger-Enquirer	Uga I w/cheerleader float (1)
Scott Conroe	Uga V in Homecoming parade (5)
Cotton States Insurance	Program ad (5)
Jack Davis	Herschel Heisman poster (4); Bill Hartman drawing, Sonny *SI* cover (5)
Steve Deal	Pandemonium in Jacksonville (3)
Dog Magazine	Uga V on cover (5)
Dog Fancy	Magazine cover, "100 Moments" clip (4)
Billy Downs	Feted at Capitol (3)
Wingate Downs	Herschel Walker vs. Notre Dame (3)
Drinnon	Little girl w/cheerleaders (1)

Paul Efland, UGA Photographic Services	Tuxedo (1); Uga Cam (5); Seilers at Alumni Club, Baxter Street Esplanade (6)
Travis Ellison	Sonny at stadium, majorette (2); giving Sonny "sugar", Sara and Bess w/young Uga V (5); Sonny running Uga III (6)
Dan Evans	WTOC broadcaster, Santa Claus, Goldberg, GameDay crew (5); Harrick, Uga VI w/basketball cheerleader, Sonny thumb's-up sign (6)
Rick Fiala	Warhol Bulldogs (6)
Peter Frey, UGA Photographic Services	Girl at Picture Day (6)
Georgia Magazine	Sonny and Uga II on cover, *GM* Web page, Patrick Dean cartoon (5)
Wilton Hall	Cheerleader Billy Coven (1)
Kent Hannon	Dog bowl, "Finish the Drill," Picture Day, Uga VI at airport, dogtag (Prologue); spiked collar (1); SUV, sawhorse, Big Dog, ceramic bowl, vanity plates (2); Otto gravestone (4); patting the dog, bird girl (5); Blake, Dooley at Picture Day, tailgate, Swann setup, Cecelia SUV, student photo day, Sonny portrait, Seilers at Butts-Mehre, Seilers' award, Dawg crossing, Seilers' backdoor, Uga VI w/blanket (6)
Laura Heath	*Midnight* stars on stage (5)
Hill's Pet Nutrition	Hollett portrait/ad brochure (2)
Phyllis Kandal	Gov. Harris w/team, w/Sonny & Uga IV (4)
Richard Kolb	Uga II under table (2)
Hugh Maddox	Uga VI w/Hairy Dawg after dark (6)
McDonald's	Uga V ad (5)
Perry McIntyre	Starter portrait, Herschel Walker vs. Notre Dame (3); Albuquerque Final Four, Buzz (4); Sonny portraits (6)
Randy Miller	Mesh jersey (1); Smokey (3); granite bulldog, media frenzy (5)
Walker Montgomery	Vet student (1); Swann at college, Uga III retires (3)
Montgomery Advertiser	Uga V lunge (5)
Radi Nabulsi	*SI* medallion (5); media frenzy, Uga V sundown profile (6)
Rick O'Quinn, UGA Photographic Services	Uga IV funeral (4); Uga V funeral (5); Uga VI's entrance, collar changing, girls at Picture Day (6)
Pandora	Arch, Co-op, Sigma Chi float, Sigma Chi sweetheart, Dean Tate, bugle, 1892 team, 1929 Yale ticket, boy at stadium, Ty Cobb, Uga I-II (1)
Pollack & Daly	Dooley on players' shoulders (2)
Random House	*Midnight* cover (4)
Becky Reid	Memorial Hall statue, gravestone (1); Bobby Lenihan, gravestone (2); gravestone (3); gravestone (4); starter portrait, gravestone (5); Speaker Murphy, Dooley statues, Frobus portrait, Kathy Pulliam (6)

Rem	Uga w/kennel (2)
Manny Rubio	Herschel in huddle, running, w/"Walkerville" sign (4)
Savannah Evening Press	Oranges clip, men on couch (1)
Savannah Morning News	"Paws & Effect" (5); D.C. clip (6)
Rachel Smith	Sonny on The Ref
Sports Illustrated	Herschel Walker story (3); Best Mascot page, *Midnight* premier page (5)
William Taggart	Men on couch (1)
Chris Taylor	Beauty queen (6)
UGA Publications	UGA phone book cover (5)
UGA Sports Communications	Starter portrait, 1943 Rose Bowl, Cheerleader Hannah Jones, Mike w/Carol Ann Conner, Nancy Butts w/Uga I, Wally Butts photo, stretch jersey, '62 Homecoming queen Emma Jo Jones, '64 game program, oil painting (1); starter portrait, changing of collar, Ann DeLong, '67 game program, '68 SEC champs, Mike Cavan, Charles giving Uga III ice, modern fireplug, Uga V w/doghouse, Knapp/Magillicuddy I (3); starter portrait, Cecelia trying collar on Uga IV, Bess/Sara w/Uga IV, Marty Argo, Herschel Walker w/Heisman, Herschel Walker w/Sonny/Uga IV, Seilers on game program, Uga IV w/cast, Otto in game jersey, Tim Worley, Uga IV in Red Cross shirt, retiring Dooley (4); Uga IV w/Magillicuddy I, Uga V as a pup, bronze bulldog, Uga V-VI face to face (5); starter portrait, Adams changing collar, golf brochure, Gym Dogs poster, Dooley w/Uga III, Picture Day outdoors, bath time, living room memorabilia, family portrait, Uga VI w/cheerleader (6)
University Woman's Club	*The Little Bulldog* (4)
Warner Brothers	Movie poster, *Midnight* stills (5)
Washington Post	Uga I retirement clip (1)
Danny White	Middle linebacker, Uga III on ice (3); Uga IV portrait (4)
Joe Whiteko	Sports South, broadcaster near doghouse, Uga V w/girl (5); Charles w/film crew, platform w/Uga VI (6)
The Seilers	All other photos/memorabilia not noted

Index

People